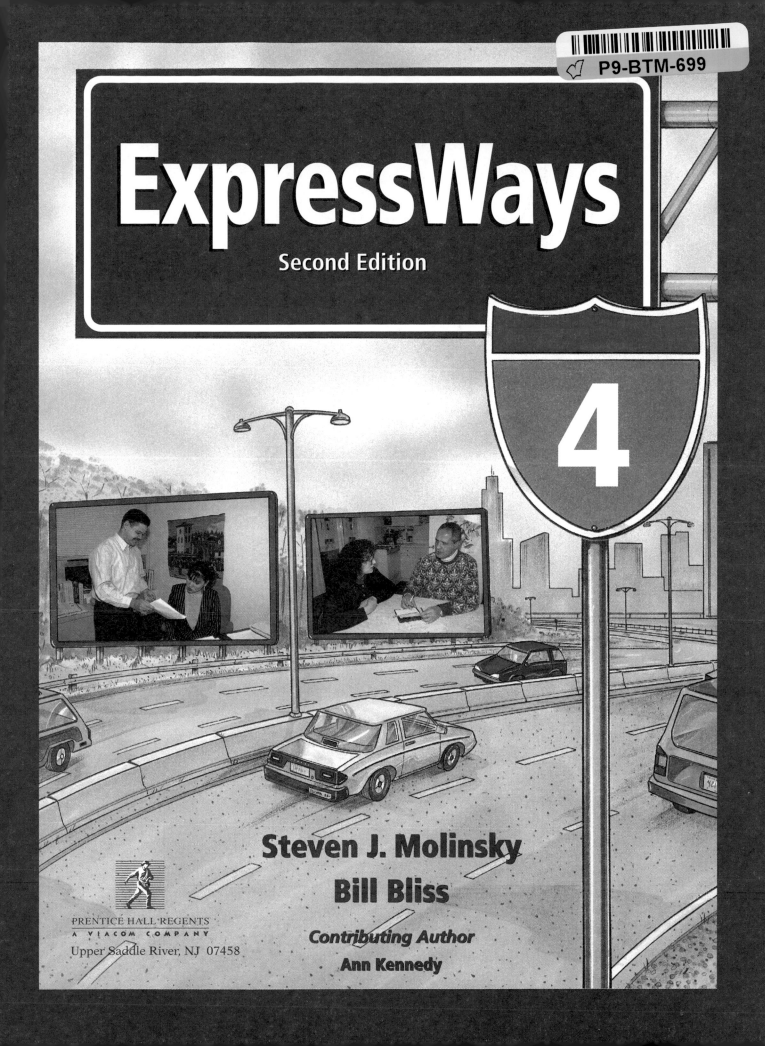

ExpressWays

Second Edition

4

Steven J. Molinsky

Bill Bliss

Contributing Author

Ann Kennedy

PRENTICE HALL REGENTS
A VIACOM COMPANY
Upper Saddle River, NJ 07458

Molinsky, Steven J.
    ExpressWays 4 / Steven J. Molinsky, Bill Bliss ; contributing
author, Ann Kennedy.
        p.   cm.

    Includes index.
    ISBN 0-13-385759-X.
    1. English language– –Textbooks for foreign speakers.   I. Bliss,
Bill. II. Kennedy, Ann. III. Title: ExpressWays four
PE1128.M6755   1996
428.2'4– –dc20   96-20553
                                                   CIP

Publisher: *Louisa B. Hellegers*
Production Supervision/Compositors: *Ken Liao, Jan Sivertsen*
Composition Support: *Christine Mann*
Manufacturing Manager: *Ray Keating*
Electronic Image Production Supervisor: *Todd Ware*
Electronic Image Production/Scanning: *Marita Froimson*
Electronic Art: *Marita Froimson / Ken Liao / Jan Sivertsen*
Art Director: *Merle Krumper*
Interior Design: *PC&F / Wanda España*
Photographer: *Paul Tañedo*
Acknowledgments: p.108, (top) *Virginia Glass Factory* by Lewis W. Hines (Museum of the City of New York, Riis P);
(bottom) *Sweat Shop* (Brown Brothers)

Illustrator: *Richard Hill*

The authors gratefully acknowledge the contribution of Tina Carver
in the development of the *ExpressWays* program.

© 1997 by PRENTICE HALL REGENTS
Prentice-Hall, Inc.
A Simon & Schuster Company
Upper Saddle River, New Jersey 07458

Printed in the United States of America

10 9 8 7 6 5 4 3 2 1

ISBN   0-13-385759-X

Prentice-Hall International (UK) Limited, *London*
Prentice-Hall of Australia Pty. Limited, *Sydney*
Prentice-Hall Canada Inc., *Toronto*
Prentice-Hall Hispanoamericana, S.A., *Mexico*
Prentice-Hall of India Private Limited, *New Delhi*
Prentice-Hall of Japan, Inc., *Tokyo*
Simon & Schuster Asia Pte. Ltd., *Singapore*
Editora Prentice-Hall do Brasil, Ltda., *Rio de Janeiro*

EXPRESSWAYS 4 TRAVEL GUIDE

EXIT 4 • Rules and Regulations At School — 67

EXIT 7 • Friends, Family, and Co-Workers   135

ExpressWays is a comprehensive 4-level course for learners of English. Its innovative spiraled curriculum integrates lifeskill topics, functions, and grammar in an imaginative highway theme that puts students *in the fast lane* for an exciting and motivating journey to English language proficiency.

The program consists of the following components:

- **Student Texts** — offering speaking, reading, writing, and listening comprehension practice that integrates grammar and functions in a topic-based curriculum.

- **Activity Workbooks** — offering reinforcement through grammar, reading, writing, and listening comprehension practice fully coordinated with the student texts. The activity workbooks also feature dynamic exercises in pronunciation, rhythm, stress, and intonation.

- *Navigator* **Companion Books** — visually exciting "magazine-style" texts, offering a complete lifeskill curriculum fully integrated with the *ExpressWays* student texts.

- **Teacher's Guides** — providing background notes and expansion activities for all lessons and step-by-step instructions for teachers.

- **Audio Program** — offering realistic presentations of conversations, listening comprehension exercises, and readings from the student texts and workbooks.

- **Picture Program** — featuring Picture Cards for vocabulary development, enrichment exercises, and role-playing activities.

- **Placement and Achievement Testing Program** — providing tools for the evaluation of student levels and progress.

The *ExpressWays* series is organized by a spiraled curriculum that is covered at different degrees of intensity and depth at each level. *ExpressWays 1* and *2* provide beginning-level students with the most important vocabulary, grammar, and functional expressions needed to communicate at a basic level in a full range of situations and contexts. *ExpressWays 3* and *4* cover the same full range of situations and contexts, but offer intermediate-level students expanded vocabulary, more complex grammar, and a wider choice of functional expressions.

The Dimensions of Communication: Function, Form, and Content

ExpressWays provides dynamic, communicative practice that involves students in lively interactions based on the content of real-life contexts and situations. Every lesson offers students simultaneous practice with one or more functions, the grammatical forms needed to express those functions competently, and the contexts and situations in which the functions and grammar are used. This "tri-dimensional" clustering of function, form, and content is the organizing principle behind each lesson and the cornerstone of the *ExpressWays* approach to functional syllabus design.

ExpressWays offers students broad exposure to uses of language in a variety of relevant contexts: in community, school, employment, home, and social settings. The series gives students practice using a variety of registers, from the formal language someone might use in a job interview, with a customer, or when speaking to an authority figure, to the informal language someone would use when talking with family members, co-workers, or friends.

A special feature of the course is the treatment of discourse strategies — initiating conversations and topics, hesitating, asking for clarification, and other conversation skills.

An Overview

Chapter-Opening Photos

Each chapter-opening page features two photographs of situations that depict key topics presented in the chapter. Students make predictions about who the people are and what they might be saying to each other. In this way, students have the opportunity to share what they already know and to relate the chapter's content to their own lives and experiences.

Guided Conversations

Guided conversations are the dialogs and exercises that are the central learning devices in *ExpressWays*. Each lesson begins with a model conversation that depicts a real-life situation and the vocabulary, grammar, and functions used in the communication exchange. Key functional expressions in the models are in boldface type and are footnoted, referring students to short lists of alternative expressions for accomplishing the functions. In the exercises that follow, students create new conversations by placing new content into the framework of the model, and by using any of the alternative functional expressions.

Original Student Conversations

Each lesson ends with an open-ended exercise that offers students the opportunity to create and present original conversations based on the theme of the lesson. Students contribute content based on their experiences, ideas, and imaginations.

Follow-Up Exercises and Activities

A variety of follow-up exercises and activities reinforce and build upon the topics, functions, and grammar presented in the guided conversation lessons.

- **Constructions Ahead!** exercises provide focused practice with grammar structures.

- **CrossTalk** activities provide opportunities for students to relate lesson content to their own lives.

- **InterActions** activities provide opportunities for role playing and cooperative learning.

- **InterView** activities encourage students to interview each other as well as people in the community.

- **Community Connections** activities provide task-based homework for students to get out into their communities to practice their language skills.

- **Cultural Intersections** activities offer rich opportunities for cross-cultural comparison.

- **Figure It Out!** activities offer opportunities for problem-solving.

- **Your Turn** activities provide opportunities for writing and discussion of issues presented in the chapter.

- **Listening Exercises** give students intensive listening practice that focuses on functional communication.

- **Reflections** activities provide frequent opportunities for self-assessment, critical thinking, and problem-solving.

- **Reading** passages in every chapter are designed to provide interesting and stimulating content for class discussion. These selections are also available on the accompanying audiotapes for additional listening comprehension practice.

InterChange

This end-of-chapter activity offers students the opportunity to create and present "guided role plays." Each activity consists of a model that students can practice and then use as a basis for their original presentations. Students should be encouraged to be inventive and to use new vocabulary in these presentations and should feel free to adapt and expand the model any way they wish.

Rest Stop

These "free role plays" appear after every few chapters, offering review and synthesis of the topics, functions, and grammar of the preceding chapters. Students are presented with eight scenes depicting conversations between people in various situations. The students determine who the people are and what they are talking about, and then improvise based on their perceptions of the scenes' characters, contexts, and situations. These improvisations promote students' absorption of the preceding chapters' functions and grammar into their repertoire of active language use.

Support and Reference Sections

End-of-Chapter Summaries include the following:

- **Looking Back** — a listing of key functional expressions in the chapter for review.

- **Construction Sign** — a listing of the key grammar structures presented in the chapter.

- **ExpressWays Checklist** — a self-assessment listing of key lifeskills presented in the chapter.

An **Appendix** provides charts of the grammar constructions presented in each chapter, along with a list of cardinal numbers, ordinal numbers, and irregular verbs.

An **Index** provides a convenient reference for locating topics and grammar in the text.

Suggested Teaching Strategies

We encourage you, in using *ExpressWays*, to develop approaches and strategies that are compatible with your own teaching syle and the needs and abilities of your students. While the program does not require any specific method or technique in order to be used effectively, you may find it helpful to review and try out some of the following suggestions. (Specific step-by-step instructions may be found in the *ExpressWays* Teacher's Guides.)

Chapter-Opening Photos

Have students talk about the people and the situations and, as a class or in pairs, predict what the characters might be saying to each other. Students in pairs or small groups may enjoy practicing role plays based on these scenes and then presenting them to the class.

Guided Conversations

1. SETTING THE SCENE: Have students look at the model illustration in the book. Set the scene: Who are the people? What is the situation?
2. LISTENING: With books closed, have students listen to the model conversation — presented by you, by a pair of students, or on the audiotape.
3. CLASS PRACTICE: With books still closed, model each line and have the whole class practice in unison.
4. READING: With books open, have students follow along as two students present the model.

5. PAIR PRACTICE: In pairs, have students practice the model conversation.

6. ALTERNATIVE EXPRESSIONS: Present to the class each sentence of the dialog containing a footnoted expression. Call on different students to present the same sentence, replacing the footnoted expression with its alternatives. (You can cue students to do this quickly by asking, "What's another way of saying that?" or "How else could he/she/you say that?")

7. EXERCISE PRACTICE: (optional) Have pairs of students simultaneously practice all the exercises, using the footnoted expressions or any of their alternatives

8. EXERCISE PRESENTATIONS: Call on pairs of students to present the exercises, using the footnoted expressions or any of their alternatives.

Original Student Conversations

In these activities, which follow the guided conversations at the end of each lesson, have students create and present original conversations based on the theme of the lesson. Encourage students to be inventive as they create their characters and situations. (You may ask students to prepare their original conversations as homework, then practice them the next day with another student and present them to the class. In this way, students can review the previous day's lesson without actually having to repeat the specific exercises already covered.)

CrossTalk

Have students first work in pairs and then share with the class what they talked about.

InterActions

Have pairs of students practice role playing the activity and then present their role plays to the class.

InterView

Have students circulate around the room to conduct their interviews, or have students interview people outside the class. Students should then report to the class about their interviews.

Community Connections

Have students do the activity individually, in pairs, or in small groups and then report to the class.

Cultural Intersections

Have students do the activity in class, in pairs, or in small groups.

Reflections

Have students discuss the questions in pairs or small groups, and then share their ideas with the class.

Your Turn

This activity is designed for both writing practice and discussion. Have students discuss the activity as a class, in pairs, or in small groups. Then have students write their responses at home, share their written work with other students, and discuss in class. Students may enjoy keeping a journal of their written work. If time permits, you may want to write a response to each student's journal, sharing your own opinions and experiences as well as reacting to what the student has written. If you are keeping portfolios of students' work, these compositions serve as excellent examples of students' progress in learning English.

Reading

Have students discuss the topic of the reading beforehand, using the pre-reading questions suggested in the Teacher's Guide. Have students then read the passage silently, or have them listen to the passage and take notes as you read it or play the audiotape.

InterChange

Have students practice the model, using the same steps listed above for guided conversations. Then have pairs of students create and present original conversations, using the model dialog as a guide. Encourage students to be inventive and to use new vocabulary. (You may want to assign this exercise as homework, having students prepare their conversations, practice them the next day with another student, and then present them to the class.) Students should present their conversations without referring to the written text, but they should also not memorize them. Rather, they should feel free to adapt and expand them any way they wish.

Rest Stop

Have students talk about the people and the situations, and then present role plays based on the scenes. Students may refer back to previous lessons as a resource, but they should not simply re-use specific conversations. (You may want to assign these exercises as written homework, having students prepare their conversations, practice them the next day with another student, and then present them to the class.)

We hope that *ExpressWays* offers you and your students a journey to English that is meaningful, effective, and entertaining. Have a nice trip!

Steven J. Molinsky
Bill Bliss

A **model conversation** offers initial practice with the functions and structures of the lesson.

Key functional expressions are in boldface type and are footnoted, referring students to a box containing alternative expressions for accomplishing the functions.

In the **exercises**, students create new conversations by placing new content into the framework of the model, and by using any of the alternative functional expressions.

The **open-ended exercise** at the end of each lesson asks students to create and present original conversations based on the theme of the lesson.

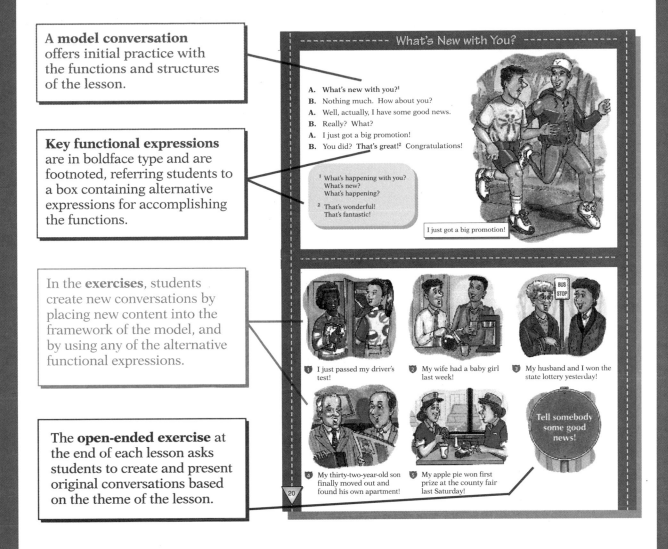

------- What's New with You? -------

A. What's new with you?[1]
B. Nothing much. How about you?
A. Well, actually, I have some good news.
B. Really? What?
A. I just got a big promotion!
B. You did? **That's great!**[2] Congratulations!

[1] What's happening with you?
What's new?
What's happening?

[2] That's wonderful!
That's fantastic!

I just got a big promotion!

1 I just passed my driver's test!

2 My wife had a baby girl last week!

3 My husband and I won the state lottery yesterday!

4 My thirty-two-year-old son finally moved out and found his own apartment!

5 My apple pie won first prize at the county fair last Saturday!

Tell somebody some good news!

20

For example:

Exercise 1 might be completed by placing the new exercise content into the existing model:

A. What's new with you?
B. Nothing much. How about you?
A. Well, actually, I have some good news.
B. Really? What?
A. I just passed my driver's test!
B. You did? That's great! Congratulations!

Exercise 2 might be completed by using the new exercise content and some of the alternative expressions:

A. What's happening with you?
B. Nothing much. How about you?
A. Well, actually, I have some good news.
B. Really? What?
A. My wife had a baby girl last week!
B. She did? That's wonderful! Congratulations!

Sometimes the footnote indicates that an alternative expression requires a change in the grammar of the sentence. For example, the sentences:

Let's ____! = Let's go swimming!
Why don't we ____? = Why don't we go swimming?

ExpressWays

Second Edition

4

Exit 1

FRIENDS AND NEIGHBORS

Take Exit 1 to . . .

→ Greet someone and introduce yourself, using noun clauses

→ Ask for information about a neighborhood, using embedded questions

→ Ask permission to do something

→ Offer to help someone, using gerunds

→ Ask a favor of someone

→ Give advice about home repairs, using *should* and gerunds

→ Inquire about home repair services, using embedded questions

→ Discuss home repairs, using embedded questions

Functions This Exit!

Greeting People
Offering to Help
Appreciation
Permission
Requests
Advice–Suggestions
Asking for and Reporting
Information

Gloria has just moved into Michael's building. She's asking him a question about one of the rules of the building. What do you think they're saying to each other?

Vincent is having a problem with something in his house. He's calling his neighbor David and is asking him for advice. What do you think Vincent and David are saying to each other?

A. Oh, hello. You must be our new neighbor.

B. Yes, that's right.

A. Let me introduce myself. I'm Jane, your neighbor across the street.

B. **Nice to meet you.**[1] **My name is**[2] Wendy.

A. Tell me, when did you move in?

B. Yesterday.

A. Well, **if there's anything I can do to help,**[3] please let me know.

B. Thanks very much. **I appreciate it.**[4]

---

[1] It's nice to meet you.
Nice meeting you.
It's nice meeting you.
I'm glad to meet you.

[2] I'm

[3] if I can help in any way
if I can be of any help

[4] I appreciate that.
That's very kind of you.

our new neighbor

Yesterday.

Wendy

Jane, your neighbor across the street

the new person in Apartment 42 — *Two days ago.*

Diane

1 Jeff, your neighbor across the hall

the new tenant — *This morning.*

Mrs. Baxter

2 Frank, the building superintendent

the new occupant — *Yesterday afternoon.*

Bill Davis

3 Hector, your mail carrier

the person who bought the Wilsons' house — *Last weekend.*

Maria Sanchez

4 Thelma Wagner, your neighbor down the block

new here — *The day before yesterday.*

Walter

5 Max, the president of the condo* association

Greet a new neighbor. Introduce yourself and offer help.

* condo = condominium

Who Are They?

1. This is Sam. He's the superintendent.   _This is Sam, the superintendent._

2. I'm Mrs. Wong. I'm the new English teacher.   _____

3. She's Mrs. Wagner. She's Robert's mother.   _____

4. This is Tiger. He's our favorite cat.   _____

5. Meet the Ortegas. They're our upstairs neighbors.   _____

It's About Time

Choose the correct time expression.

1. Our new neighbors moved in ____.
   a. tomorrow morning
   b. the day before yesterday *(circled)*
   c. in a few weeks

2. Eileen started working here ____.
   a. now
   b. next week
   c. two weeks ago

3. We've been living here in Dallas ____.
   a. since last year
   b. right now
   c. before

4. I haven't seen your sister ____.
   a. for a long time
   b. tomorrow afternoon
   c. yesterday

5. Are you going on vacation ____?
   a. before
   b. next week
   c. in a long time

6. We haven't seen our neighbors ____.
   a. yesterday
   b. in a long time
   c. about an hour ago

7. I don't think we've met ____.
   a. before
   b. a year ago
   c. at the last meeting

8. I'm sure I'll get promoted ____.
   a. last month
   b. in a month
   c. in the past month

CrossTalk

Have a "neighborly" chat with a partner. Ask each other:

> How well do you know your neighbors?
> How often do you see them?
> Do you ever help your neighbors? How?
> Do they ever help you? How?
> What kind of relationship do you think
>   neighbors should have with each other?

Report to the class about your discussion and compare people's experiences.

A. Excuse me.[1] I'm sorry to bother you. **Could you possibly tell me**[2] when they pick up the garbage?

B. Yes. They pick it up on Friday mornings.

A. On Friday mornings?

B. **That's right.**[3] Are you new here?

A. Yes. I just moved in.

[1] Pardon me.

[2] Could you please tell me
Could you tell me

[3] Uh-húh.

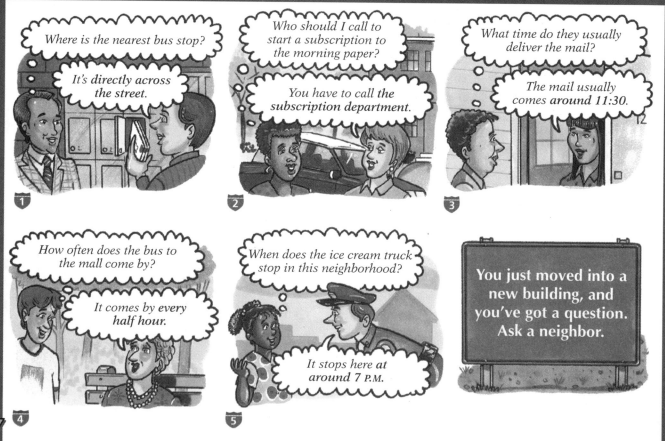

A. **Pardon me.**[1] I hate to bother you. **Could you please tell me**[2] **if**[3] there's a post office nearby?

B. Yes. There's a post office two blocks up the street.

A. Two blocks up the street?

B. Uh-húh.[4] Are you new here?

A. Yes. I just moved in.

[1] Excuse me.

[2] Could you possibly tell me
Could you tell me

[3] whether

[4] That's right.

1

2

3

4

5

You just moved into a new building, and you've got a question. Ask a neighbor.

Constructions Ahead!

"Where is the bus stop?" "What are they doing?" "Who should I call?"	Could you tell me { where the bus stop is? what they're doing? who I should call?
"What time does the mail arrive?" "Where do they live?" "Why did they move?"	Could you tell me { what time the mail arrives? where they live? why they moved?

1 What time is it?

Could you tell me ____what time it is____ ?

2 Where is the nearest laundromat?

Could you possibly tell me _____ ?

3 What are you doing?

Can you tell me _____ ?

4 Why can't we park there?

Could you tell me _____ ?

5 When does the bus get here?

Do you know _____ ?

6 Where does the superintendent live?

Can you please tell me _____ ?

7 How long did the Petersons live here?

Do you happen to know _____ ?

8 Who is the president of the condo association?

Can you please tell me _____ ?

"Is there a post office nearby?"	Could you tell me { if / whether } there's a post office nearby?
"Do they allow parking here?"	Could you tell me { if / whether } they allow parking here?

9 Is there a park in this neighborhood?

Can you tell me _____ ?

10 Does the mail come before noon?

Do you know _____ ?

11 Are you allowed to hang clothes here?

Could you tell me _____ ?

12 Do the neighbors get together very often?

Do you know _____ ?

13 Are there a lot of rules in the building?

Can you please tell me _____ ?

14 Can we put plants on the balcony?

Could you please tell me _____ ?

15 Do you have any more questions?

Can you tell me _____ ?

Listen

Listen and choose the best response.

1 a. Yes. They are.
   (b.) Yes. There are.
   c. Yes. You are.

2 a. Yes. It's at the next intersection.
   b. Yes. There is.
   c. Yes. It is.

3 a. No. It isn't.
   b. No. There isn't.
   c. No. You can't.

4 a. Yes. You do.
   b. Yes. The superintendent.
   c. Yes. You should.

5 a. Yes. On the third floor.
   b. Yes. He is.
   c. Yes. You can.

6 a. Yes. I mailed it already.
   b. Yes. I already knew that.
   c. Yes. It came around noon.

Fill It In!

Fill in the correct answer.

1 Could you please tell me ____?
   a. where's the playground located
   b. if the playground is located
   (c.) where the playground is located

2 Could you possibly tell me ____?
   a. whether there's a mailbox nearby
   b. where's a mailbox
   c. if is there's a mailbox nearby

3 Could you tell me ____?
   a. what time does the supermarket close
   b. when does the supermarket close
   c. what time the supermarket closes

4 Would you happen to know ____?
   a. we're allowed to park here
   b. if we're allowed to park here
   c. whether are we allowed to park here

5 Do you know ____?
   a. who's the owner of the building
   b. the owner of the building is
   c. who the owner of the building is

6 Could you tell me ____?
   a. can we leave our bicycles here
   b. if we can leave our bicycles here
   c. where can we leave our bicycles

7 Would you know ____?
   a. how much the rent is
   b. how much is the rent
   c. whether the rent is

8 Could you please tell me ____?
   a. why have they sold the building
   b. why they've sold the building
   c. if have they sold the building

InterActions

The conversations on pages 4 and 5 all end with the two neighbors saying:

> *Are you new here?*

> *Yes. I just moved in.*

With a partner, choose one of these situations and continue the conversation between the two new neighbors — any way you wish. What other questions do they ask each other? How does each conversation end? Present your scenes to the class and compare with other students' versions of the same situations.

A. Are you allowed to[1] park in front of the building?

B. Yes, you are.

A. Thanks.

A. Is it okay to[2] leave a bicycle in the hallway?

B. No, it isn't.

A. Oh, okay. Thanks.

[1] Are you permitted to
Yes, you are.
No, you aren't.

[2] Is it all right to
Yes, it is.
No, it isn't.

Ask if you're allowed to do something.

8

Fill It In!

Fill in the correct answer.

1. Is it okay to have pets _____?
   a. up the street
   b. in the dormitory *(circled)*
   c. late at night

2. Are you permitted to use _____?
   a. the bus stop
   b. on the roof
   c. the fireplace

3. You're allowed to play _____.
   a. pets
   b. music in your office
   c. bicycle

4. I'm going to leave my bicycle _____.
   a. on the balcony
   b. in the fireplace
   c. in the garbage chute

5. Throw it down _____.
   a. the dormitory
   b. the garbage chute
   c. the laundry

6. Can you park _____?
   a. on the balcony
   b. in front of the dormitory
   c. in the fireplace

Listen

Listen and choose the correct answer.

1. a. you aren't.
   b. you are. *(circled)*

2. a. it isn't.
   b. it is.

3. a. it isn't.
   b. you aren't.

4. a. you are.
   b. it is.

5. a. there are.
   b. you can.

6. a. you aren't.
   b. you don't.

7. a. you can.
   b. you can't.

8. a. it is.
   b. you are.

Missing Lines

Complete the following conversation any way you wish and then present it to the class.

A. I have a few questions about the rules of the building.

B. Certainly. What are your questions?

A. Are you allowed to . . . . ?

B. Yes, you are.

A. Oh, good. And are you permitted to . . . . . .
. . . . ?

B. No, you aren't. . . . . .ing is
definitely not permitted.

A. Also, I'm wondering if it's okay to . . . .
. . . . ?

B. No, it isn't.

A. I see. And are you allowed to . . . . ?

B. No. I'm afraid you aren't. Do you have any other questions?

A. No, I guess not.

Do You Want Any Help?

A. Do you want any help[1] carrying those grocery bags upstairs?

B. Sure. **If you don't mind.**[2]

A. No, not at all. **I'd be glad to give you a hand.**[3]

B. Thanks. I appreciate it.

---

[1] Do you need any help
Can I give you a hand

[2] If you wouldn't mind.
If it's no trouble.

[3] I'd be happy to give you a hand.
I'd be glad to help.
I'd be happy to help.

carry those grocery bags upstairs

1 tune up your car

2 take out the garbage

3 lift that couch up the steps

4 rake the leaves

5 put up that TV antenna

A neighbor might need help doing something. Offer to help.

What's the Answer?

Choose the correct word and practice the conversation with another student.

A. Do you need any help (take ⟨taking⟩)[1] that sofa up the steps?

B. Sure. If you (would   wouldn't)[2] mind.

A. No, not at all. (I   I'd)[3] be happy to give you a (hand   help)[4]. Do you want any help (moving   move)[5] anything else?

B. Well, you could (help   hand)[6] me (carry   upstairs)[7] these boxes, if you (don't   didn't)[8] mind.

A. No. (I'm   I'd)[9] be glad to.

B. Thanks. I (appreciate   appreciating)[10] it.

A. My pleasure.

Fill It In!

Fill in the correct answer.

1 _____ tuning up your car?
  a. Do you need any
  b. Can I give you
  c. Do you want any help *(circled)*

2 Can I _____?
  a. help you rake
  b. want any help raking
  c. happy to help you rake

3 Do you want _____?
  a. helping taking that out
  b. taking that out
  c. help taking that out

4 _____ happy to carry those bags.
  a. I
  b. I'd be
  c. If it's

5 Do you _____ taking out the trash?
  a. need any help
  b. have a hand
  c. carry

6 Can I _____ you a hand?
  a. help
  b. mind
  c. give

InterActions

Try an experiment! Offer to help several people do things.

    What's their reaction?
    How do they express their appreciation?
    How do you feel after you've helped them?

Share your experiences with the class.

Do you need any help?

A. Could I ask you a favor?[1]

B. What is it?

A. Could you possibly[2] lend me a cup of sugar?

B. Okay.[3]

A. Are you sure? I don't want to trouble you.

B. No problem. **I'd be happy to.**[4]

A. Thanks. I appreciate it.

> [1] Could you do me a favor?
> Could you do a favor for me?
>
> [2] Could you please
> Could I ask you to
> Do you think you could
>
> [3] All right.
> Sure.
> Of course.
>
> [4] I'd be glad to.

lend me a cup of sugar

1 pick up our mail while we're away

2 help me jump-start my car

3 let me borrow your laptop computer

4 give me a lift downtown

5 watch Jeremy for a few minutes while I run to the grocery store

Ask a favor of someone.

Listen

Listen and choose the correct answer.

1
 a. hand
 b. help
 c. favor *(circled)*

2
 a. help
 b. a favor
 c. be willing to help

3
 a. problem you
 b. no trouble
 c. trouble you

4
 a. be willing to help
 b. do us a favor
 c. favor please

5
 a. ask me a favor
 b. help me
 c. trouble me

6
 a. happy to trouble you
 b. thanks
 c. glad to

The Best Response

Choose the best response for Speaker B.

1 A. Could you do a favor for me?
 B. a. Are you sure?
  b. I don't want to trouble you.
  c. Of course. *(circled)*

2 A. Could you possibly lend me your Walkman?
 B. a. What is it?
  b. I'd be glad to.
  c. If you don't mind.

3 A. I don't want to trouble you.
 B. a. No problem.
  b. Sure.
  c. If it's no trouble.

4 A. Do you think you'd be able to jump-start my car?
 B. a. I appreciate it.
  b. I don't want any trouble.
  c. Sure. Where is it?

5 A. I'd be glad to.
 B. a. What is it?
  b. Thanks.
  c. No problem.

6 A. Could I ask you to watch our house while we're away?
 B. a. Can I give you a hand?
  b. All right.
  c. If it's no trouble.

7 A. Could you do me a favor?
 B. a. Not at all.
  b. Yes. You are.
  c. Sure. What is it?

8 A. Could you give me a lift?
 B. a. I'd be glad to lift it.
  b. Of course. Where are you going?
  c. That's very kind of you.

CrossTalk

Talk with a partner about doing favors.

Do you often ask people to do favors for you?
What kinds of favors have you asked people to do?
How do you feel when you ask someone to do you a favor?
How does it feel when another person asks you to do a favor?

Report to the class about your discussion and compare experiences.

Could I ask you a favor?

A. I'm having a problem with my radiator.

B. What's wrong?

A. There's no heat coming out of it.

B. **How about**[1] turning the valve a few times?

A. I've tried turning the valve a few times, but that didn't work.

B. Well . . . **How about**[1] kicking it?

A. I've tried kicking it, but that didn't work either.

B. **Can I offer you some advice?**[2]

A. Sure. What?

B. **I think you should**[3] call the superintendent.

A. You're probably right.

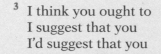

---

[1] What about

[2] Can I offer you a piece of advice?
Can I offer you a suggestion?

[3] I think you ought to
I suggest that you
I'd suggest that you

turn the valve a few times
kick it
call the superintendent

1 tighten the bulb
replace the bulb
call an electrician

2 adjust the antenna
play with the knobs on the back of the set
call a TV repair shop

3 jiggle the handle
lift up the ball in the tank
call a plumber

You've got a home repair problem. Ask a friend for suggestions.

Matching Lines

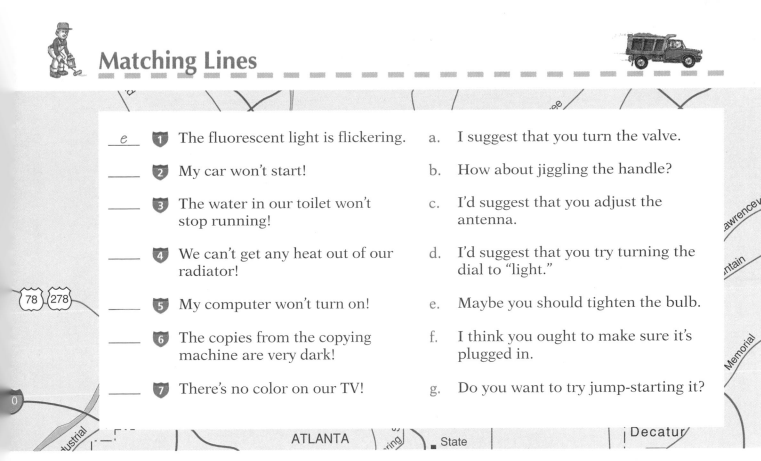

____e____ **1** The fluorescent light is flickering.

a. I suggest that you turn the valve.

____ **2** My car won't start!

b. How about jiggling the handle?

____ **3** The water in our toilet won't stop running!

c. I'd suggest that you adjust the antenna.

____ **4** We can't get any heat out of our radiator!

d. I'd suggest that you try turning the dial to "light."

____ **5** My computer won't turn on!

e. Maybe you should tighten the bulb.

____ **6** The copies from the copying machine are very dark!

f. I think you ought to make sure it's plugged in.

____ **7** There's no color on our TV!

g. Do you want to try jump-starting it?

Listen

Listen and decide which of the following is having the problem.

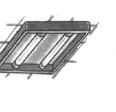   

____   ____   __1__   ____   ____

CrossTalk

Brainstorm with a partner suggestions for solving the following household problems. Then compare with other students' solutions.

- You can't turn your shower off, and water is leaking everywhere!
- Your cassette player won't go in reverse.
- Your gas stove doesn't have any flame.
- Your kitchen sink is clogged.
- Your front doorbell is stuck! It keeps making a humming sound.

15

A. County Plumbing and Heating.

B. Hello. **Could you tell me**[1] if you fix kitchen sinks?

A. Yes. What's the problem?

B. Water is leaking all over my kitchen floor.

A. Well, we can send one of our plumbers at 4:00 this afternoon. Will someone be home then?

B. At 4:00 this afternoon? I'll be here.

A. What's the name?

B. Charles Franklin.

A. And the address?

B. 74 College Street.

A. Phone number?

B. 396-2465.

A. All right, Mr. Franklin. We'll have a plumber there at 4:00 this afternoon.

B. Thanks very much.

[1] Can you tell me

Do you fix kitchen sinks?

Water is leaking all over my kitchen floor.

plumber
4 o'clock this afternoon

Charles Franklin
74 College Street
396-2465

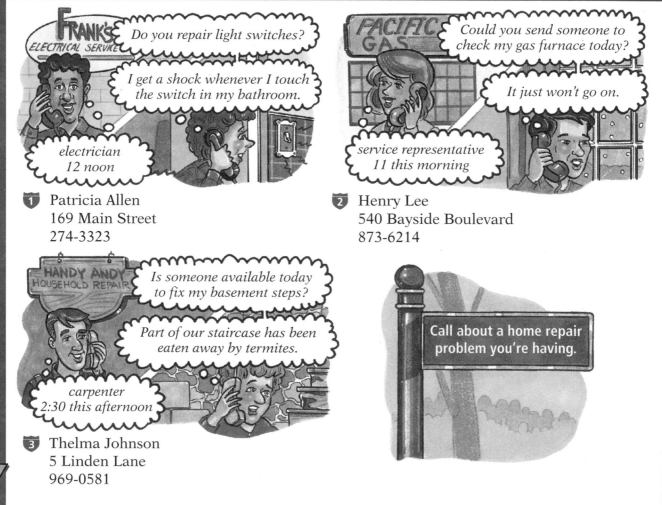

Do you repair light switches?

I get a shock whenever I touch the switch in my bathroom.

electrician
12 noon

1 Patricia Allen
169 Main Street
274-3323

Could you send someone to check my gas furnace today?

It just won't go on.

service representative
11 this morning

2 Henry Lee
540 Bayside Boulevard
873-6214

Is someone available today to fix my basement steps?

Part of our staircase has been eaten away by termites.

carpenter
2:30 this afternoon

3 Thelma Johnson
5 Linden Lane
969-0581

Call about a home repair problem you're having.

Who Will They Send?

| a carpenter | an electrician | a plumber |
| a painter | a mechanic | a service representative |

1 We've tried everything, but our furnace isn't working!

We'll send _a service representative_ as soon as possible.

2 Water is leaking all over the bathroom floor!

We can send —————— to your home this afternoon.

3 Our lamps are flickering on and off!

Well, we can send —————— to your home tomorrow morning.

4 We need to fix the steps to our attic.

We'll send —————— sometime next Monday.

5 The paint on the outside of our house is chipping off!

We can send —————— to your home next Wednesday.

6 I've tried jump-starting it, but it still won't start!

We'll send —————— as soon as possible.

Community Connections

Complete the following and then share with other students in your class.

When I have electrical problems, I call . . . .

When I have plumbing problems, I call . . . .

When I have heating problems, I call . . . .

When I need household repairs, I call . . . .

When my TV isn't working right, I call . . . .

Many homeowners hire contractors to do their household repairs. Professional painters paint the inside of homes. Professional carpenters fix steps and repair doors. Plumbers fix problems with toilets and sinks. And electricians repair problems with light switches and water heaters. However, many homeowners do these types of repairs themselves. They enjoy the work so much that many of them do their own home improvements, too.

There are many resources available that make these kinds of *do-it-yourself* jobs easy to do. Book stores and libraries carry many books and magazines that offer suggestions and ideas for home repairs and improvements. There are also videocassettes and TV shows that give complete instructions for building cabinets, putting tile in bathrooms, installing windows, and even building additional rooms to enlarge a home. There are also programs that show how to wax wooden floors, clean fireplaces, and paint decorative designs on walls. Local colleges and high schools offer adult education classes in the evenings and on weekends. In these classes, people can learn such things as techniques for building furniture and porches, ways to set up a solar heating system, and procedures for saving energy in the home.

When homeowners are ready to begin their projects, they can go to their neighborhood hardware store to find many of the tools and supplies they need. These small stores sell all kinds of tools — from hammers and saws to shovels and wrenches. They also carry electrical wire, paintbrushes, toilet parts, and many types of wallpaper and colors of house paint.

Some hardware stores are larger than the typical neighborhood store. They look like warehouses and sell many things at discount prices. In addition to the merchandise available at the smaller hardware stores, most of these larger stores also sell doors, windows, easy-to-assemble furniture, and lumber. Some also carry large plants and trees and other big items, such as lawnmowers and children's swing sets. Customers can get a lot of help at these large stores. There are guide books on wallpapering, housepainting, carpentry, plumbing, and electrical wiring. The employees are usually happy to offer information and suggestions.

With a few necessary tools, some good instructions, and a little patience, do-it-yourself homeowners can become amateur electricians, plumbers, carpenters, and painters. Finishing a household repair or improvement gives them a great sense of accomplishment and the satisfaction of learning a new skill. And since they pay for only the materials and not for the labor, do-it-yourself homeowners are happy to see how much money they can save!

True or False?

1. Many homeowners don't hire professionals to do their household repairs.

2. According to the reading, some hardware stores offer classes on making home improvements.

3. *Do-it-yourself* homeowners can save money.

4. The merchandise in neighborhood hardware stores is probably more expensive than the same merchandise in larger hardware stores.

5. It's very difficult to get advice on doing household repairs and improvements.

What's the Answer?

1. An example of a *contractor* is _____.
   a. a homeowner
   b. an amateur
   c. a professional repairperson

2. Books, videocassettes, and adult education classes are _____.
   a. tools for household repairs
   b. resources for homeowners interested in home improvement
   c. all available at local hardware stores

3. An example of *home improvement* is _____.
   a. repairing a light switch
   b. fixing a broken window
   c. wallpapering

4. An example of *home repair* is _____.
   a. painting decorative designs on walls
   b. fixing a broken toilet
   c. asking advice from a professional

5. An amateur carpenter is not _____.
   a. a professional carpenter
   b. an adult
   c. a homeowner

6. When you do your own repairs, you usually _____.
   a. hire contractors
   b. pay for labor costs to do improvements on your home
   c. save money

Your Turn

For Writing and Discussion

Write a description of how to fix something — for example, a broken doorbell, a light that is flickering, or even a car that won't start because the battery is dead. Give specific step-by-step instructions. Then present your "do-it-yourself" repairs, and as a class, publish a **Guide to Home Repairs.**

I Think I've Figured Out What the Problem Is

A. Well, Mr. Prescott. I think I've figured out what the problem is with your hot water heater.

B. Oh? What?

A. The thermostat is burned out.

B. The thermostat is burned out? Hmm. What needs to be done to fix it?

A. Well, I'm going to have to replace the thermostat and put in a few new wires.

B. Could I ask you how much that will cost?

A. Well, let me see . . . The parts will cost about forty dollars. And it should take about thirty minutes to do the work, so the labor will be about twenty-five dollars. We're talking about a total cost of about sixty-five dollars.

B. Sixty-five dollars?

A. Yes. Do you want me to go ahead and fix it?

B. I guess so.

A. Okay. I'll have your hot water heater working like new in no time at all!

A. Well, (Mr./Ms./Mrs./Miss) _____. I think I've figured out what the problem is with your _____.

B. Oh? What?

A. _____.

B. _____? Hmm. What needs to be done to fix it?

A. Well, I'm going to have to _____.

B. Could I ask you how much that will cost?

A. Well, let me see . . . The parts will cost about _____. And it should take about _____ to do the work, so the labor will be about _____. We're talking about a total cost of about _____.

B. _____?

A. Yes. Do you want me to go ahead and fix it?

B. I guess so.

A. Okay. I'll have your _____ working like new in no time at all!

Something in your home is broken. For example:

your stove   *your doorbell*   *your dishwasher*

your front light   *your television set*

You're talking with a repairperson who has come to fix it. Create an original conversation, using the model dialog above as a guide. Feel free to adapt and expand the model any way you wish.

Looking Back

Greeting People
Nice to meet you.
It's nice to meet you.
Nice meeting you.
It's nice meeting you.
I'm glad to meet you.

Offering to Help
If there's anything I can do to help, …
If I can help in any way, …
If I can be of any help, …

Do you want any help ___ing?
Do you need any help ___ing?
Can I give you a hand ___ing?

I'd be glad to give you a hand.
I'd be happy to give you a hand.
I'd be glad to help.
I'd be happy to help.

Responding to an Offer of Help
If you don't mind.
If you wouldn't mind.
If it's no trouble.

Appreciation
I appreciate it.
I appreciate that.
That's very kind of you.

Asking about Permissibility
Are you allowed to ___?
Are you permitted to ___?

Is it okay to ___?
Is it all right to ___?

Requests
Could I ask you a favor?
Could you do me a favor?
Could you do a favor for me?

Could you possibly ___?
Could you please ___?
Could I ask you to ___?
Do you think you could ___?

Responding to Requests
Okay.
All right.
Sure.
Of course.

I'd be happy to.
I'd be glad to.

Offering Suggestions
Can I offer you some advice?
Can I offer you a piece of advice?
Can I offer you a suggestion?

How about ___?
What about ___?

I think you should ___.
I think you ought to ___.
I suggest that you ___.
I'd suggest that you ___.

Asking for Information
Could you possibly tell me ___?
Could you please tell me ___?
Could you tell me ___?
Can you tell me ___?

Now Leaving Exit 1 Construction Area

- [ ] **Embedded Questions**
- [ ] **Gerunds**
- [ ] **Infinitives**
- [ ] **Noun Clauses**
- [ ] **Time Expressions**

Sorry for the inconvenience. For more information see page 180.

ExpressWays Checklist

I can . . .

- [ ] Greet someone and introduce myself
- [ ] Ask for information about a neighborhood
- [ ] Ask permission to do something
- [ ] Offer to help someone
- [ ] Ask a favor of someone
- [ ] Give advice about home repairs
- [ ] Inquire about home repair services
- [ ] Discuss home repairs

22

Exit 2

CALLING PEOPLE GOING PLACES

Take Exit 2 to . . .

➤ Learn how to make different kinds of telephone calls, using imperatives

➤ Call for transportation and recreation reservations, using embedded questions and short answers

➤ Make person-to-person collect calls

➤ Understand transportation safety rules, using imperatives and reported speech

➤ Ask about transportation, using embedded questions

➤ Leave telephone messages, using noun clauses and embedded questions

Functions This Exit!

Asking for and Reporting Information
Attracting Attention
Want–Desire
Offering to Help
Offering to Do Something
Initiating Conversations
Checking and Indicating Understanding
Asking for Repetition
Apologizing
Instructing

Amy is talking to an airline ticket agent on the telephone. What do you think they're saying to each other?

Emily is leaving a message for Alice, who isn't there. What do you think Emily and the person who has answered the phone are saying to each other?

- *Pick up the receiver.*
- *Drop the money in the coin slot.*
- *Wait for the dial tone and dial.*

use this pay phone

A. Excuse me. **Could you please tell me**[1] how to use this pay phone?

B. Sure. Pick up the receiver. Drop the money in the coin slot. Then, wait for the dial tone and dial. **Have you got it?**[2]

A. I think so. **Let me see.**[3] First, I pick up the receiver.

B. Yes.[4]

A. Then, I drop the money in the coin slot. Right?

B. Uh-húh.[4]

A. Hmm. I forgot the last part. What am I supposed to do after that?

B. You wait for the dial tone and dial.

A. Okay. **Now I've got it.**[5] Thanks very much.

---

[1] Could you possibly tell me
Could I ask you to tell me

[2] Do you follow me?
Okay?

[3] Let me see if I understand.
Let me see if I've got that.

[4] Um-hḿm.
That's right.

[5] Now I understand.
Now I see.

A. Excuse me. **Could you please tell me**[1] how to _____?

B. Sure. _____.

_____.

Then, _____.

Have you got it?[2]

A. I think so. **Let me see.**[3] First, I _____.

B. Yes.[4]

A. Then, I _____. Right?

B. Uh-húh.[4]

A. Hmm. I forgot the last part. What am I supposed to do after that?

B. You _____.

A. Okay. **Now I've got it.**[5] Thanks very much.

- _Dial "one."_
- _Dial the area code._
- _Dial the seven-digit local phone number._

1 make a long-distance call

- _Insert your bank card face up into the slot._
- _Enter your personal identification number._
- _Indicate the amount you want, and wait for the money to come out._

2 use this cash machine

- _Press down on the clutch when you start the engine._
- _Push the stick to the forward left position to get into first gear._
- _Start driving, and use the clutch and stick to shift into "second" and "third" as you pick up speed._

3 use the stick-shift car I just rented

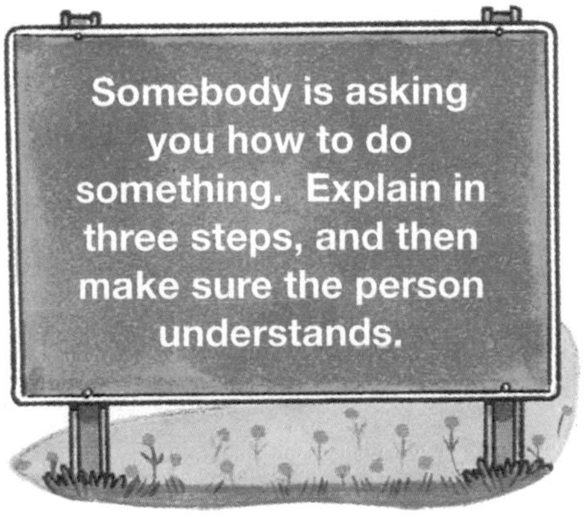

Somebody is asking you how to do something. Explain in three steps, and then make sure the person understands.

Fill It In!

Fill in the correct answer.

1. _____ the engine.
  a. Indicate
  b. Do
  c. Start ⓒ

2. _____ the area code.
  a. Dial
  b. Insert
  c. Wait

3. _____ the money in the coin slot.
  a. Dial
  b. Shift
  c. Drop

4. _____ the call now.
  a. Do
  b. Make
  c. Have

5. _____ into first gear.
  a. Stick
  b. Use
  c. Shift

6. _____ your identification number.
  a. Make
  b. Enter
  c. Drop

7. _____ down on the clutch.
  a. Press
  b. Pull
  c. Get

8. Listen for the dial tone and _____.
  a. wait
  b. dial
  c. pick up the receiver

9. _____ the receiver.
  a. Press down
  b. Give
  c. Pick up

Listen

Listen and decide which statement is true.

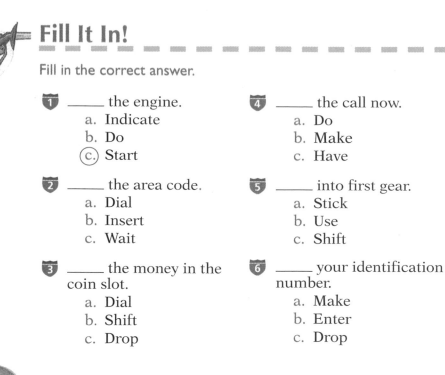

1. a. He's telling how to make a long-distance call. ⓐ
  b. He's telling how to use a pay phone.
  c. He's telling how to call the operator.

2. a. She's telling how to use an elevator.
  b. She's telling how to use a credit card to make a long-distance call.
  c. She's telling how to use a cash machine.

3. a. He's explaining how to use a stamp machine.
  b. He's explaining how to use a soda machine.
  c. He's explaining how to use a cash machine.

4. a. She's explaining how to transfer a call.
  b. She's explaining how to call the operator.
  c. She's explaining how to dial a local telephone number.

5. a. He's telling how to pick up speed.
  b. He's telling how to start a car with manual transmission.
  c. He's telling how to enter a personal identification number.

6. a. She's telling how to open a door.
  b. She's telling how to stop a stick-shift car.
  c. She's telling how to use a candy machine.

Which Word Doesn't Belong?

Circle the word that doesn't belong.

1. a. clutch   b. engine   (c.) phone   d. shift

2. a. speed   b. receiver   c. telephone   d. dial

3. a. money   b. slot   c. coins   d. cash

4. a. engine   b. motor   c. distance   d. machine

5. a. second   b. first   c. third   d. forward

6. a. tell   b. pick   c. show   d. explain

REFLECTIONS
What's your learning style? How do you prefer to learn something? Do you like to learn by yourself? Do you read instructions? Do you ask someone to help you or show you what to do? What new things have you learned to do recently, and how did you learn them?

Discuss in pairs or small groups, and then share your ideas with the class.

CrossTalk

Some people prefer to drive a stick-shift car.   *Others prefer to drive an automatic.*

Which do you prefer? Why? Can you think of some advantages and disadvantages of each? Talk with a partner and then report to the class.

Figure It Out!

Mystery Directions

With a partner, write out a set of instructions for using something—a computer, a car, a telephone, a fax machine, a washing machine at a laundromat, or something else.

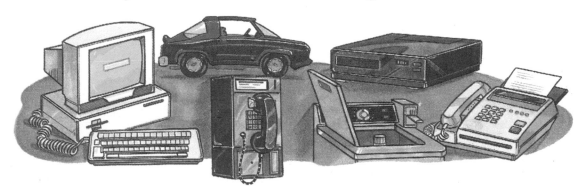

Present the instructions to the class. Can your classmates guess what the instructions are for?

A. Trans-Global Airlines. Barbara speaking. **May I help you?**[1]

B. Yes. **I'd like to know**[2] **whether**[3] you have flights between Chicago and Miami.

A. Yes, we do.

B. **I'd like to**[4] reserve two seats on your earliest flight on March 4th.

A. Hold on one moment, please, while I check to see what's available.

B. Thank you.

---

[1] Can I help you?

[2] I'd like to know _____.
Could you tell me _____?
Could you please tell me _____?

[3] if

[4] I want to

Do you have flights between Chicago and Miami?

two seats on your earliest flight on March 4th

Barbara

Are you located near the airport?

David

[1] a room with two double beds for the 9th and 10th of April

Do you take reservations?

Pierre

[2] a table for a party of six at 7:30 this evening

Is the Ice Show still in town this week?

Patty

[3] 5 seats for tomorrow afternoon's show

Is Anna-Maria Albertini performing in Carmen this weekend?

Oscar

[4] 4 seats in the first balcony for this Sunday's performance

Will ordinary citizens be allowed to fly in space someday?

Lieutenant Crandall

[5] a seat on the first flight to Mars

Call an airline, a hotel, a restaurant, or a theater, and ask for information.

* NASA = National Aeronautics and Space Administration

28

Fill It In!

Fill in the correct answer.

1 I'd like to reserve a table for ____ of ten for 8:00 tonight.
   a. performance
   b. seats
   c. a party *(circled)*

2 We'd like to know what time ____ leaves.
   a. the reservation
   b. the next flight
   c. tomorrow

3 Could you tell me where the restaurant is ____?
   a. nearby
   b. this weekend
   c. located

4 Could you please hold ____ for a moment?
   a. in
   b. on
   c. at

5 Is Lorenzo Scavarotti ____ tonight?
   a. performance
   b. performing
   c. perform

6 I want to know how long the show will be ____.
   a. earliest
   b. in town
   c. performance

7 I'd like to know whether we can ____ two tickets for tomorrow's show.
   a. reservation
   b. allowed
   c. reserve

8 I'd like to get two tickets in the first ____.
   a. balcony
   b. seat
   c. table

Listen

Listen and decide what place these people are calling.

| *a hotel* | *a theater* | *an airline* | *a post office* | *a restaurant* | *a service station* |
| _____ | _____ | __1__ | _____ | _____ | _____ |

Community Connections

Look in your local newspaper, and make a list of local events taking place in your community this week. Call if you have any questions about these events. Report to the class what you discovered.

A. Operator.

B. **I'd like to**[1] make this a person-to-person collect call, please.

A. What's the name of the person you're calling?

B. Carl Hendricks.

A. And your name?

B. Bob Pickerton.

A. **Excuse me.**[2] **Did you say**[3] "Bickerton" with a "B"?

B. No. "Pickerton" with a "P."

A. All right. One moment, please.

> [1] I want to
>
> [2] I'm sorry.
>
> [3] Was that

Bob Pickerton is calling Carl Hendricks.

1 Nancy Sack is calling Ethel Martin.

2 Albert Tennyson is calling Michael Chang.

3 Peter Halston is calling Ms. Walker.

4 Norton is calling Ralph.

5 Mrs. Fogel is calling Mr. Simpson.

Make a person-to-person collect call.

Listen

Listen and finish the sentence.

hair air	double trouble	Fix Six

1. (a.) conditioner fixed.
   b. cut.

2. a. beds.
   b. you.

3. a. the TV picture, please.
   b. tickets cost $12.00.

thirty dirty	drink rink	serve reserve

4. a. tickets available?
   b. clothes in the washer?

5. a. open today?
   b. delicious?

6. a. four seats for tonight's show?
   b. this order right away?

café coffee	tables tablets	sticks six

7. a. maker on sale?
   b. nearby?

8. a. will help your cold.
   b. are reserved.

9. a. tickets that I reserved?
   b. of butter out of the refrigerator?

Crossed Lines

Oh, no! There's a problem with the telephone. Put the following lines in the correct order.

____ Excuse me. Was that "Yaffey" with a "Y"?

____ Wanda Hall.

____ All right. One moment, please.

____ I want to make this a person-to-person collect call.

____ And your name?

____ What's the name of the person you're calling?

____ George Jaffey.

_1_ Operator.

____ No. "Jaffey" with a "J."

A. Excuse me.[1] Please fasten your seat belt.

B. I'm sorry.[2] I didn't hear you. What did you say?[3]

A. I asked you to fasten your seat belt.

B. Oh, okay.

A. Excuse me.[1] Please don't play your radio on the bus.

B. I'm sorry.[2] I didn't hear you. What did you say?[3]

A. I asked you not to play your radio on the bus.

B. Oh, okay.

[1] Pardon me. [2] Sorry. [3] Could you repeat that?
Would you repeat that?
Could you say that again?
Would you say that again?

1

2

3

4

5

Give someone a transportation safety warning.

Constructions Ahead!

> "Please fasten your seat belt."   I asked you to fasten your seat belt.
> "Please don't stand there."   I asked you not to stand there.

1 **A.** Please keep your seat belt on.
B. Excuse me. I didn't hear you. What did you say?
A. I asked you _to keep your seat belt on._

2 **A.** Please don't play music after 10:00.
B. Excuse me. Could you say that again?
A. I asked you _____.

3 **A.** Please put your box in the overhead rack.
B. Pardon me. I didn't hear you. What did you say?
A. I asked you _____.

4 **A.** Could you give these menus to table three?
B. Sorry. Would you say that again?
A. I asked you _____.

5 **A.** Don't leave your bicycle in the hallway.
B. Sorry. Could you say that again?
A. I asked you _____.

6 **A.** Please don't eat on the subway.
B. What did you say?
A. I asked you _____.

CrossTalk

Talk with a partner about the reasons for various safety rules. For example:

Why should you fasten your seat belt on an airplane?
Why shouldn't people be allowed to play radios loudly on buses or airplanes?
Why is it dangerous to lean against the doors on the subway?
Why is it important to put things in the overhead rack on a train or airplane?

Report back to the class and compare everybody's ideas.

A. Excuse me.[1] Do you by any chance know[2] what our expected arrival time in Denver is?

B. We're due to arrive at 3 P.M.

A. At 3 P.M.?

B. Yes. That's right.

A. Thank you.

[1] Pardon me.

[2] Would you by any chance know
Do you by any chance happen to know
Would you by any chance happen to know
Could you possibly tell me
Could you please tell me

What is our expected arrival time in Denver?

We're due to arrive at 3 P.M.

What's the weather forecast for the weekend?

We're expecting temperatures in the 80s.

1

Is the dining car still open?

I'm afraid it closed ten minutes ago.

2

Will there be a place to get something to eat at our next stop?

There's a snack bar next to the bus station.

3

Is St. Louis one hour ahead of or behind New York?

It's an hour behind.

4

When are we going to cross the International Date Line?

In an hour or so.

5

You're on a plane, train, bus, or boat, and you have a question.

What's the Question?

1. Could you please tell me ____?
   - a. when we're expected to arrive
   - b. when are we expected to arrive
   - c. when do we expect to arrive

2. Would you by any chance know ____?
   - a. what time is it in Tokyo
   - b. what time it's in Tokyo
   - c. what time it is in Tokyo

3. Do you happen to know ____?
   - a. what tonight's homework
   - b. what is tonight's homework
   - c. what tonight's homework is

4. Do you by any chance know ____?
   - a. what time they'll be home
   - b. when will they be home
   - c. when will be they home

5. Do you by any chance happen to know ____?
   - a. if are we going to arrive on time
   - b. if we're going to arrive on time
   - c. if we going to arrive on time

6. Could you possibly tell me ____?
   - a. where I can get something to eat
   - b. where do I get something to eat
   - c. where can I get something to eat

7. Would you by any chance know ____?
   - a. whether's the dining car open
   - b. whether is the dining car open
   - c. whether the dining car is open

8. Could you tell me ____?
   - a. who's the manager
   - b. who the manager is
   - c. who the manager

9. Would you by any chance happen to know ____?
   - a. how long we'll be circling over the airport
   - b. how long be circling over the airport
   - c. how long will we be circling over the airport

InterActions

Work with a group of students in your class to create a scene on a bus, train, plane, or boat.
One of you is either a driver, conductor, pilot, flight attendant, or captain—depending on the type
of transportation. The others are passengers. On this particular day, the passengers have LOTS of
questions:

> *Do you by any chance know . . . ?*

> *Would you by any chance know . . . ?*

> *Could you please tell me . . . ?*

> *Would you by any chance happen to know . . . ?*

> *Could you possibly tell me . . . ?*

Present your "transportation scenes" to the class. Which group has the most questions? Which
questions are the most interesting? the most unusual?

A. Hello. **May I please speak to**[1] Mr. Lawrence?

B. I'm afraid he isn't here right now. **Can I take a message?**[2]

A. Yes. This is Joe from the repair shop. I'm calling to tell him his car is ready.

B. Okay. I'll give him the message.

A. Thanks.

[1] Can I please speak to

[2] Can I give *him* a message?
Would you like to leave a message?

Mr. Lawrence
Joe from the repair shop

1 Mrs. Jenkins
her lawyer, Mr. Carter

2 Robert
his accountant, Mrs. Santiago

3 Mr. or Mrs. Lane
Mr. Grimes, the landlord

4 Lance
Max, his agent

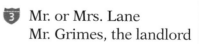

5 the president
Martha Porter of Topeka, Kansas

Call someone and leave a message. You have something to tell that person.

A. Hello. **I'd like to speak to Julie.**[1]

B. I'm afraid she isn't here right now. **Can I take a message?**[2]

A. Yes. This is her friend Mark. I'm calling to ask her **if**[3] she'd like to see a movie tomorrow night.

B. Okay. I'll give her the message.

A. Thanks.

[1] I'd like to speak to _____, if *she's* there.

[2] Can I give *her* a message?
Would you like to leave a message?

[3] whether

Would you like to see a movie tomorrow night?

Julie
her friend Mark

Can you give me a ride home from work today?

1 Michael Rogers
his friend Steve

What is the answer to Question 5 on tonight's math homework?

2 Debbie
Bobby

Where did you leave the car keys?

3 Ms. Donaldson
her husband

Do you know what time the school board meeting starts tonight?

4 Maria
Kathy Nelson

Who is your veterinarian?

5 Mr. or Mrs. Jenkins
Oliver Smith, their upstairs neighbor

Call someone and leave a message. You have something to ask that person.

37

Constructions Ahead!

> "Your car is ready."
> "You forgot to pay your rent."
>
> "Would you like to see a movie?"
> "Can you give me a ride home?"
>
> I'm calling to tell him his car is ready.
> I'm calling to tell them they forgot to pay their rent.
>
> I'm calling to ask her if she'd like to see a movie.
> I'm calling to ask him whether he can give me a ride home.

1. I'm calling to ask David ____.
   a. he wants to go to the ballgame
   b. if he'd like to go to the ballgame
   c. does he want to go to the ballgame

2. I'm calling to tell you ____.
   a. when will my plane arrive
   b. whether arrive my plane
   c. when my plane will arrive

3. Can I ask you ____?
   a. why you're leaving so early
   b. why are you leaving so early
   c. if you're leaving so early

4. I'm calling to tell you ____.
   a. where is the party
   b. whether the party
   c. where the party is

5. I'm calling to ask ____.
   a. what time the play starts
   b. when does the play start
   c. whether the play starts

6. I'm calling to tell you ____.
   a. can I come to your party
   b. I can't come to your party
   c. if can I come to your party

A Telephone Call

Choose the correct word. Then practice the conversation with a partner.

A. Hello. (Would (Can))[1] I please speak to Mrs. Mangini?

B. Yes. (May Do)[2] I ask (is who who's)[3] calling?

A. This is Bob Simmons from the EMP Corporation.

B. I'm (hearing afraid)[4] her phone is busy.
Would you like to (hold talk)[5]?

A. I'd prefer to (take give)[6] her a message.

B. Just (an hour a moment)[7], please. Okay. I can
(take give)[8] your message now.

A. I'm calling to (speak tell)[9] her
(if the meeting the meeting)[10] for this afternoon
has been canceled.

B. Okay. I'll (give take)[11] her the message.

Another Telephone Call

Choose the correct word. Then practice the conversation with a partner.

A. Hello. (I (I'd))[1] like to speak to Ms. Nelson, (please   thanks)[2].

B. She isn't here right now. (Can   Would)[3] you like to (take   leave)[4] a message (for   to)[5] her?

A. Yes. This is Ann Porter. I'm calling to (tell   ask)[6] her if (she'd   she'll)[7] like to meet for dinner this evening.

B. All right. I'll give (him   her)[8] the message.

Listen

Listen and complete the message.

1

To _Mrs. Robertson_
Date _____ Time _____
While You Were Out
M _Fred_
of _Joe's Garage_
Phone _____
          AREA CODE   NUMBER   EXTENSION

TELEPHONED	✓	PLEASE CALL	
WAS IN TO SEE YOU		WILL CALL AGAIN	
WANTS TO SEE YOU		URGENT	
RETURNED YOUR CALL			

MESSAGE _____
_____ Your car is ready. _____

2

To _Mr. Jenkins_
Date _____ Time _____
While You Were Out
M _Jeff Carter_
of _Ace Corporation_
Phone _____
          AREA CODE   NUMBER   EXTENSION

TELEPHONED	✓	PLEASE CALL	
WAS IN TO SEE YOU		WILL CALL AGAIN	
WANTS TO SEE YOU		URGENT	
RETURNED YOUR CALL			

MESSAGE _____
_____
_____
_____

3

To _Ms. Rodriguez_
Date _____ Time _____
While You Were Out
M _Arthur Wong_
of _Washington College_
Phone _____
          AREA CODE   NUMBER   EXTENSION

TELEPHONED	✓	PLEASE CALL	
WAS IN TO SEE YOU		WILL CALL AGAIN	
WANTS TO SEE YOU		URGENT	
RETURNED YOUR CALL			

MESSAGE _____
_____
_____
_____

4

To _Tom Parker_
Date _____ Time _____
While You Were Out
M _Sally Langley_
of _Benton Company_
Phone _____
          AREA CODE   NUMBER   EXTENSION

TELEPHONED	✓	PLEASE CALL	
WAS IN TO SEE YOU		WILL CALL AGAIN	
WANTS TO SEE YOU		URGENT	
RETURNED YOUR CALL			

MESSAGE _____
_____
_____
_____

5

To _Mary Marx_
Date _____ Time _____
While You Were Out
M _Barbara Baxter_
of _Personnel Office_
Phone _____
          AREA CODE   NUMBER   EXTENSION

TELEPHONED	✓	PLEASE CALL	
WAS IN TO SEE YOU		WILL CALL AGAIN	
WANTS TO SEE YOU		URGENT	
RETURNED YOUR CALL			

MESSAGE _____
_____
_____
_____

6

To _Dr. Morgan_
Date _____ Time _____
While You Were Out
M _Officer Hall_
of _Westville Police Dept._
Phone _____
          AREA CODE   NUMBER   EXTENSION

TELEPHONED	✓	PLEASE CALL	
WAS IN TO SEE YOU		WILL CALL AGAIN	
WANTS TO SEE YOU		URGENT	
RETURNED YOUR CALL			

MESSAGE _____
_____
_____
_____

Telephones have changed! For many years, people rented telephones from the telephone company. Now, consumers are able to purchase their own phones at department stores, hardware stores, discount catalog stores, and electronic equipment stores.

In the past, telephones were traditionally black and had a *rotary* dialing system. Nowadays, most telephones have push-buttons, which the user presses when making a telephone call. These *touchtone* telephones come in colors to match every room of the house and are available in a variety of styles. Some phones for the bedroom include a clock radio and an alarm. There are *Big Bird* and *Mickey Mouse* phones for children. There are cordless phones that allow the user to walk around the house while talking on the phone, car phones that allow people to talk on the telephone while driving, and *flip phones* that people can carry with them wherever they go!

There are many different telephone models to select from. In traditional models, the dial and the receiver are two separate pieces. Now, one-piece phones are popular. On these phones, the receiver and the dial are contained in one unit. There are also speaker phones that allow the user to have a conversation without holding the receiver. Some phones even have a telephone *memory bank*. Frequently called numbers can be programmed into the telephone's memory and then dialed by pressing just one or two buttons. In addition, many home phones now include answering machines that automatically answer a telephone, play a message from the owner of the phone, and then record the caller's message.

Special services are available from the telephone company for an additional monthly charge. With *call waiting,* a person who is talking on the phone will hear a beep if someone else is trying to call. The person can then answer the other call while putting the first caller *on hold.* With *call forwarding,* a person can program a phone so that calls can be received at another phone number. Another special feature is *three-way calling.* This feature permits three people in different places to have a conversation together.

Telephones have changed greatly in the past few years, and they will most likely continue to change as technology becomes more and more sophisticated in the future.

True or False?

1. It's possible to buy telephones.

2. You can rent telephones at discount and electronic equipment stores.

3. In traditional model telephones, the dial and the receiver are one piece.

4. It's possible to purchase a telephone that includes an answering machine.

5. Telephone companies offer special services for a fee.

6. Telephones have become more and more sophisticated in recent years.

What's the Answer?

1. Traditional telephones had ____.
   a. push buttons
   b. answering machines
   c. a rotary dialing system

2. If certain numbers are called often, it might be a good idea to get ____.
   a. a telephone with a memory bank
   b. a telephone that includes an answering machine
   c. a flip phone

3. You can receive a telephone call at another number if you ____.
   a. use the memory bank
   b. have call forwarding
   c. dial the operator

4. If a beep is heard during a conversation, the speaker knows that ____.
   a. something is wrong
   b. someone is trying to call
   c. the line is busy

5. People who don't want to miss telephone calls when they aren't home should get ____.
   a. cordless phones
   b. special services
   c. an answering machine

6. If you don't want to use the receiver when you make a call, you should ____.
   a. get an answering machine
   b. purchase a speaker phone
   c. buy a cordless phone

CrossTalk

Discuss the following "telephone questions" with a partner.

Do you have an answering machine?
What's your opinion of answering machines?

Do you have a cordless telephone or a flip phone?
What are the advantages of these types of telephones?

Do you have call waiting or call forwarding?
What's your opinion of these types of services?

Have you ever been on a three-way call?
Tell about your experience.

Report back to the class and compare everybody's opinions.

Community Connections

Contact your local telephone company.

Ask about the different types of monthly telephone services available.
Ask how much each one costs.

Find out what special services your telephone company offers.
Find out how much each one costs.

Report back to the class and compile your findings.

Your Turn

For Writing and Discussion

Think of all the different ways people use the telephone.

You can keep in touch with friends and family members by telephone.
A great deal of business is conducted by telephone.
You can make reservations for travel and entertainment by telephone.
Many people order items from mail-order catalogs by telephone.
Others make calls to radio talk programs to express their views on current events.

Tell about the different ways you use the telephone in your daily life.

InterActions

With a partner, brainstorm what you would say if you called the president or prime minister of your country.

What questions do you have?
What opinions would you like to express?

Then, create a role play: call the president or prime minister! Present your role play to the class.

Figure It Out!

Imagine what telephone service will be like in the future. Describe it, and draw a picture of what you think the telephone of the future will look like.

Please Leave Your Name and Message

A. Hello. This is Steve. I'm not home right now. At the sound of the tone, please leave your name and message, and I'll call you back. [BEEP!]

B. Hello, Steve? This is Carol. I'm calling to ask you if you'd be interested in going to the museum with me tomorrow. Give me a call when you can. I'll be home this evening after nine. Bye.

A. Hello. This is Steve. I'm not home right now. At the sound of the tone, please leave your name and message, and I'll call you back. [BEEP!]

B. Hello, Steve? This is Dad. I'm calling to tell you Mom and I will be arriving this Monday at 7 P.M. on Trans-Global Airlines, and we want to know if you could meet us at the airport. Give us a call when you can. We'll be home all weekend. Bye.

A. Hello. This is _____. I'm not home right now. At the sound of the tone, please leave your name and message, and I'll call you back. [BEEP!]

B. Hello, _____? This is _____. I'm calling to ask/tell you _____
_____.
Give me a call when you can. I'll be home _____.
Bye.

Someone you are calling isn't home right now. Using the model dialog above as a guide, leave a message on his or her answering machine. Feel free to adapt and expand the model any way you wish.

Asking for Information
I'd like to know _____.
Could you tell me _____?
Could you please tell me _____?
Could you possibly tell me _____?
Could I ask you to tell me _____?

Do you by any chance know _____?
Would you by any chance know _____?
Do you by any chance happen to know _____?
Would you by any chance happen to know _____?

Attracting Attention
Excuse me.
Pardon me.

Want-Desire
I'd like to _____.
I want to _____.

Offering to Help
May I help you?
Can I help you?

Offering to Do Something
Can I take a message?
Can I give (him/her) a message?
Would you like to leave a message?

Initiating Conversations
May I please speak to _____?
Can I please speak to _____?

I'd like to speak to _____.
I'd like to speak to _____, if (he's/she's) there.

Checking Someone's Understanding
Have you got it?
Do you follow me?
Okay?

Checking Your Own Understanding
Let me see.
Let me see if I understand.
Let me see if I've got that.
Did you say _____?
Was that _____?

Indicating Understanding
Yes.
Uh-húh.
Um-hḿm.
That's right.

Now I've got it.
Now I understand.
Now I see.

Asking for Repetition
What did you say?
Could you repeat that?
Would you repeat that?
Could you say that again?
Would you say that again?

Apologizing
Sorry.
I'm sorry.

Now Leaving Exit 2 Construction Area

☐ **Embedded Questions**
☐ **Reported Speech**
☐ **Noun Clauses**
☐ **Imperatives**
☐ **Time Expressions**

Sorry for the inconvenience. For more information see page 181.

ExpressWays Checklist
I can . . .

☐ Make different kinds of telephone calls
☐ Call for transportation and recreation reservations
☐ Make person-to-person collect calls
☐ Understand transportation safety rules
☐ Ask about transportation
☐ Leave telephone messages

Exit 3

PERSONAL FINANCES

Take Exit 3 to . . .

→ Discuss family budgeting, using *should* and *have to*

→ Discuss paying bills, using time expressions

→ Discuss balancing a checkbook

→ Complain about mistakes on bills, using the passive voice

→ Learn about banking practices and procedures, using embedded questions

→ Discuss loan applications, using embedded questions

→ Evaluate the affordability of items, using the present perfect tense

→ Provide information for a credit card application

Functions This Exit!

Remembering/Forgetting
Asking for and Reporting
 Information
Advice–Suggestions
Obligation
Certainty/Uncertainty
Initiating a Topic
Hesitating
Checking and Indicating
 Understanding
Likes/Dislikes
Agreement/Disagreement

Susan and Peter are talking about how much cash they need to get at the bank for the weekend. What do you think they're saying to each other?

Jeff is talking to a bank officer about taking out a loan. What do you think Jeff and the bank officer are saying to each other?

A. I'm going out to do a few errands.

B. Oh. **You know what?**[1] **Maybe you should**[2] stop at the bank and get some cash.

A. Okay. How much should I get?

B. Well, let's see. **We have to**[3] buy groceries for the weekend, and we're planning to see a movie tomorrow night. You should probably get about eighty dollars.

A. Eighty dollars? Do you think that'll be enough?

B. I think so.

[1] You know something?
You know?

[3] We've got to
We need to

[2] Maybe you ought to
You should probably
It might be a good idea to

$80

buy groceries for the weekend
see a movie tomorrow night

$65

1 get more diapers
drive to Oakwood to see
your parents

$25

2 give the kids their
allowance
go bowling tonight

$95

3 pick up some stationery
supplies
take the staff out to lunch

$70

4 buy a wedding present for
your sister
take the children for
haircuts

$1500

5 pay the gardener
fly to Honolulu for the
weekend

Decide how much cash to get at the bank.

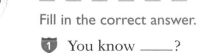

Fill It In!

Fill in the correct answer.

1 You know _____?
   (a.) what
   b. that
   c. thing

2 I'm going _____ a few errands.
   a. to make
   b. out to do
   c. off to do

3 Maybe you _____ pick up some groceries.
   a. should probably
   b. ought to
   c. have

4 It _____ a good idea to get some diapers.
   a. might be
   b. should be
   c. has to be

5 Maybe you _____ buy some bread.
   a. might
   b. ought
   c. should

6 I'm planning to _____ some cash.
   a. buy
   b. get
   c. do

Listen

Listen and fill in the amounts of money you hear.

Family Budget for the Week

Groceries: _$90_
Entertainment: _____
Kids' allowances: _____
Child care: _____
TOTAL: _____

Family Budget for the Month

Rent: _____
Utilities: _____
Telephone: _____
Credit card: _____
Insurance: _____
Tuition: _____
TOTAL: _____

Cultural Intersections

The family in Situation 2 on page 46 is discussing their children's allowance — the spending money they give to their children every week or month. Is this common in your country? Do children receive an allowance from their parents? In your opinion, should children be expected to do chores around the house in exchange for their allowance? What are the advantages of giving children an allowance? What are the disadvantages?

REFLECTIONS
Do you plan your expenses carefully? Do you make a budget for yourself or your family? How can you plan more carefully?

Discuss in pairs or small groups, and then share your ideas with the class.

A. Did you remember to[1] pay the gas bill?

B. The gas bill? No, I haven't paid that yet. It isn't due for a while.

A. Are you **sure?**[2]

B. Yes. I'm **sure.**[2] Look! Here's the bill. It says: "Due on January 15th."

A. Oh, okay. I just thought I'd remind you.

B. Thanks.

[1] Did you happen to remember to

[2] positive
certain

1.

2.

3.

4.

5.

Remind someone to pay a household bill!

Fill It In!

Fill in the correct answer.

| June 5, 1999 = 6/5/99 or 06/05/99 |

Piedmont County
Utility Services Division

Account number	122-2-725-5
Water/1000 gal.	.93
Present reading:	09/05/99
Amount due:	46.77
Payment by:	10/15/99

1. This bill is for _____.
   a. electricity
   b. telephone
   c. water (circled)

2. The payment is due on _____.
   a. September 5th
   b. 46.77
   c. October 15th

3. The total amount due is _____.
   a. 93 cents
   b. $46.77
   c. $1000.00

Listen

Listen and choose the correct date.

1. a. May 12th (circled)
   b. May 10th

2. a. February 18th
   b. February 8th

3. a. September 7th
   b. September 11th

4. a. November 30th
   b. November 13th

5. a. May 3rd
   b. May 5th

6. a. September 6th
   b. December 6th

7. a. July 9th
   b. July 19th

8. a. August 4th
   b. October 4th

REFLECTIONS
Are your utility bills high? How can you conserve water, electricity, and other forms of energy to help the environment and lower your utility bills?

Discuss in pairs or small groups, and then share your ideas with the class.

Missing Lines

Complete the following conversation between two roommates. Then with a partner, present your conversation to the class.

A. Did you remember to pay the electric bill?

B. ....

A. It was due on July 15th.

B. ....

A. You mean you forgot to pay it?!

B. ....
   What's going to happen?

A. ....

B. ....

A. I'm having trouble balancing the checkbook.

B. Oh. I forgot to tell you. I wrote a check to "Discount Shoes" for Jeffrey's sneakers.

A. Oh. I see.

B. Sorry. **I completely forgot.**[1]

A. That's okay. **Do you remember**[2] how much it was for?

B. Hmm. **Let me think for a minute.**[3] **As far as I remember,**[4] it was for thirty-six dollars.

A. Okay. Thanks.

[1] I forgot all about it.
It completely slipped my mind.

[2] Do you happen to remember

[3] Let me see.
Let's see.

[4] If I remember correctly,

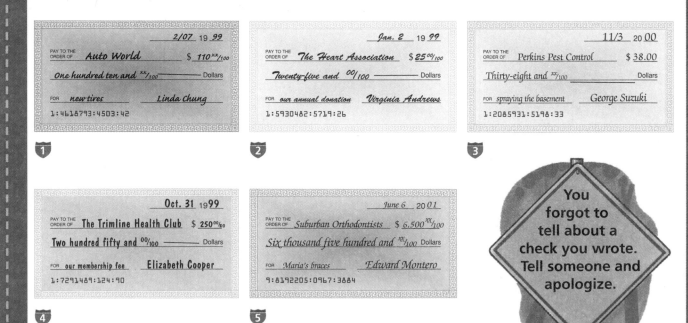

You forgot to tell about a check you wrote. Tell someone and apologize.

Fill It In!

Fill in the correct answer.

1 It completely _____. I'm really sorry.
   a. forgot
   b. remembered
   c. slipped my mind ⟲

2 I feel terrible. I forgot _____.
   a. about it
   b. correctly
   c. all

3 Hmm. Let me _____.
   a. remember
   b. forget
   c. think

4 Honey, do you _____ where it is?
   a. happen
   b. think
   c. remember

5 _____ remember, it was due on May 1st.
   a. When I
   b. As far as I
   c. Let me

6 I completely _____.
   a. think so
   b. remember
   c. forgot

7 _____ to remember how much they cost?
   a. Do you
   b. Let me
   c. Do you happen

8 Let me _____ for a minute.
   a. think
   b. see
   c. remember

Listen

Listen and put the number under the correct bill.

THE CITY GAZETTE *Newspaper*	MetroElectric	Suburban Telephone	City Cable
16.00 *due* 11/05/99 THANK YOU	From: Sep 1 To: Sep 30 Amount: 83.50 Account Number 31 47 0805	Account 201 638 6432 **May 20 1999** Currrent Charges: 21.87 MCI 5.83 Pay Suburban 27.70 by Jun 19	Account No. **1592856** Statement Date **07/25/98** Amt. of Last Payment **26.75** Payment Due **08/15/98** Total Amount Due **35.75**
_____	1	_____	_____

CrossTalk

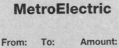

Even though it's not the most pleasant topic in the world, think for a minute about paying bills.

  Who pays the bills in your household?
  Why does that person pay the bills?
  Do you balance your checkbook?
  Do you think it's important to do this?
  Why or why not?

Talk with a partner, and then report to the class about your discussion.

A. Northwest Electric. May I help you?

B. Yes. **I believe**[1] there's a mistake on my electric bill.

A. What seems to be the problem?

B. I think I've been overcharged.

A. I see. **Could you tell me**[2] what your name is?

B. Gloria Lockwood.

A. And your account number?

B. 692-07-9943.

A. All right. Please hold while I check your account records.

B. Thank you.

[1] I think

[2] Can you tell me
Would you tell me

Northwest Electric.

overcharged

Gloria Lockwood
account number:
692-07-9943

Pacific Gas.

mistakenly charged for a service call

1 Carlos Valdez
account number:
05 0120 7027 12

Bell Atlantic.

charged for a call I didn't make

2 Henry Franklin
telephone number:
723-4431

County Water Department.

mistakenly charged a penalty fee for an overdue payment

3 Lucy Warner
account number:
27 0003 468

Southern Bell Telephone.

charged for a telegram I didn't send

4 William Park
telephone number:
829-3413

Metropolitan Cable TV.

charged for a channel we don't subscribe to

5 Rita Lambert
account number:
27431AJ

Call about a mistake on a household bill.

Constructions Ahead!

> Someone has overcharged me.   I've been overcharged.
> Someone is fixing your TV.   Your TV is being fixed.
> They shouldn't allow fishing.   Fishing shouldn't be allowed.
> My wife wrote this check.   This check was written by my wife.

1   Is someone repairing my watch?   Yes. It's __being repaired__ right now.

2   Who took this picture?   I think it __was taken__ by Uncle Charlie.

3   They shouldn't allow people to swim here.   I agree. Swimming _____.

4   Has a doctor seen you yet?   Yes. I've already _____.

5   Has somebody bought the red boots?   Yes. They've already _____.

6   Who invented this machine?   I think _____ by Edison.

7   Have you paid the baby-sitter?   Yes. She's already _____.

8   Please do your homework.   It's already _____.

9   Look at this bill! They want to charge me an additional $12.00!   _____ a penalty because last month's payment was overdue.

Listen

Listen and fill in the information.

1   Account number: 6 2 2 – 0 5 6 – 7 3 0 1

2   Telephone number: (_ _ _) _ _ _ - _ _ _ _

3   Account #: [| |]

4   Account no.: _ _ _ _ / _ _ _

5   Tel. no.: _ _ _ - _ _ _ _

6   Account #: [| | |] – [| |] – [| | | |] – [ ]

A. I'd like some information about opening a checking account.

B. A checking account? Certainly. What would you like to know?

A. **Could you tell me**[1] if there's a monthly service charge?

B. No, there isn't.

A. **I see.**[2]

B. Would you like to open a checking account with us?

A. Yes, I would.

B. All right. I'll get a form for you to fill out.

---

[1] Can you tell me _____?
I'd like to know _____.

[2] I understand.

checking account

1. savings account

2. NOW account

3. money market account

4. retirement account

5. Christmas Club account

Fill It In!

Fill in the correct answer.

1 We require a minimum _____.
   a. account
   b. money
   c. balance ⓒ

2 Is there a monthly _____?
   a. checking account
   b. service charge
   c. deposit

3 You're allowed to _____ whenever you like.
   a. withdrawal
   b. pay a penalty
   c. withdraw

4 Could you tell me what the interest _____ is?
   a. rate
   b. percent
   c. deposit

5 Can you tell me why I have to pay this penalty _____?
   a. service
   b. charge
   c. payment

6 Try not to make _____.
   a. a mistake
   b. an errand
   c. a penalty

7 I'd like to _____ a checking account.
   a. receive
   b. open
   c. make

8 Would you _____ to add money to your account?
   a. allow
   b. do
   c. like

9 The interest rate on that account is five and a half _____.
   a. months
   b. balance
   c. percent

10 I'd like to know about your _____ accounts.
   a. money market
   b. percent
   c. withdrawal

Community Connections

Visit a local bank and find out the "real" answers to the questions on page 54.

What kinds of accounts does the bank offer?

Is there a monthly service charge on a checking account?

What is the interest rate for a savings account?

Does the bank offer a second type of checking account with higher interest? What is the account called? What is the minimum balance?

How many withdrawals can you make each month from a money market account?

Are you allowed to withdraw money from a retirement account before the age of sixty-five?

Does the bank offer a Christmas Club account? How often do you have to make deposits into the account?

Report your findings to the class and compare different banks in your area.

A. May I help you?

B. Yes, please. I'd like to apply for an auto loan.

A. I see. **May I ask**[1] whether you have an account with us?

B. Yes. I have a savings account and a checking account.

A. All right. I'll give you an application form. You can fill it out here, or take it home **if you like.**[2]

> [1] Could I ask
> Could you tell me
>
> [2] if you'd like
> if you prefer
> if you'd prefer

an auto loan

1 a business loan

2 a loan

3 an education loan

4 a home improvement loan

5 a loan

Apply for a bank loan!

What's the Answer?

Choose the correct word. Then practice the conversation with a partner.

A. ((Could) May)[1] you help me?

B. (Certain   Certainly)[2].

A. I'd (want   like)[3] some information about (apply   applying)[4] for a loan.

B. I (see   ask)[5]. What kind of loan (would   could)[6] you like to apply for?

A. I'm not (understand   certain)[7].

B. Well, what do you (intend   like)[8] to use the (form   money)[9] for?

A. We (like   need)[10] the loan to build an addition to our house.

B. All right. (Do   Take)[11] a look at this form. It's for a home improvement loan. (Take   Fill)[12] it home, or you can (fill   do)[13] it out here if (you'll   you'd)[14] like.

A. Thank you.

Matching Lines

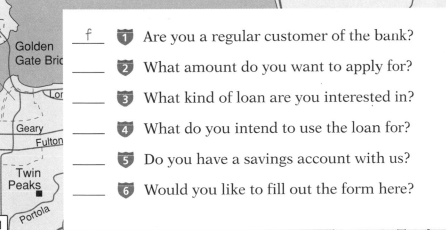

f	**1** Are you a regular customer of the bank?	a. Five thousand dollars.
___	**2** What amount do you want to apply for?	b. Yes, I do.
___	**3** What kind of loan are you interested in?	c. We'd like to take a vacation.
___	**4** What do you intend to use the loan for?	d No. I'll take it home.
___	**5** Do you have a savings account with us?	e. A business loan.
___	**6** Would you like to fill out the form here?	f. Yes. I've been coming here for ten years.

InterActions

Transform your classroom into a bank! Bring in real loan application forms, signature cards, withdrawal slips, deposit slips, and account forms. Play the roles of customers, tellers, and bank officers. Open accounts, ask for information, and apply for loans. It's a very busy day at the bank today!

A. Don't you like this rug?

B. Yes. It's very nice, but **I don't think**[1] we can afford it.

A. No?

B. No. I don't think so. Remember . . . our bank account is pretty low right now, and we still haven't paid last month's telephone bill.

A. Hmm. **You're right.**[2]

B. And besides, we don't really need a new rug right now, do we?

A. **I suppose not.**[3]

[1] I'm not sure
    I don't know if

[2] That's right.

[3] I guess not.
    Probably not.

rug

1 videocassette recorder

2 camera

3 grandfather clock

4 portable color TV

5 yacht

You'd like to buy something, but you don't think you can afford it.

What Haven't They Done?

1 Let's buy this clothes dryer. | But we still ___haven't bought___ a washer!

2 Let's pay the credit card bill. | But we still _____ this month's rent!

3 Bill wants to buy a new pair of jeans. | But he still _____ his textbooks!

4 Ann is writing a letter to her boyfriend. | But she still _____ her book report!

5 The children want to make cookies. | But they still _____ their beds!

6 I'd like you to give me my refund now. | But you still _____ me your receipt!

Can We Afford It?

Choose the correct word. Then practice the conversation with a partner,

A. I really like this car, but ((I'm not) I don't)¹ sure we (can afford   afford)² it. Remember . . . we (deposited   withdrew)³ a lot of money from our savings account last month.

B. Hmm. You're (all right   right)⁴. But (let's   let)⁵ me think for a minute. I'm (suppose   supposed)⁶ to get a promotion soon. And (when   if)⁷ I remember correctly, you (are   do)⁸, too.

A. Hmm. You're (true   right)⁹. We could (make   do)¹⁰ monthly payments, or we could (withdraw   get)¹¹ a loan. (Would   Can)¹² you prefer a dark red color?

B. I'm (don't   not)¹³ sure. Let's have lunch and talk it over.

Your Turn

For Writing and Reflection

Make a list of your monthly expenses for housing, food, transportation, clothing, and entertainment. Now evaluate your list. Are you spending too much? How can you lower your expenses? Are you saving enough money? Where do you put your savings? How can you save more? Do this every month so you can evaluate your budget.

Reading: *Credit Cards*

Credit cards are common these days. Consumers consider credit cards to be very useful and convenient. They can use their cards in many shops and restaurants. They don't need to carry large amounts of cash in their wallets or purses. And if they find themselves unexpectedly in need of money, they can use their credit cards to pay for goods and services or even to get cash advances from certain banks.

Consumers can apply for different types of credit cards. One major credit card company sends a monthly statement to the customer and requires that the total amount be paid immediately. Other major companies send a monthly statement, but only require payment of a portion of the total bill right away. Customers can pay a minimum amount shown on the bill or any larger amount they wish to pay. Many people use their credit cards this way so that they can afford to buy items they will pay for over a period of time. This can be expensive, however, because the credit card companies charge interest on the customers' unpaid balances.

Credit cards can also be very convenient for shopping by mail or telephone. Many catalogs include a place to fill in a credit card number on their order forms. By writing down the card number and signing on the appropriate line, a person can charge the purchase to his or her credit card account. Customers can also use credit cards to purchase items by telephone. They order merchandise and give their credit card number over the phone. The order is mailed to their home address, and the charges appear on their next monthly credit card bill.

Although credit cards can be very convenient, they can also cause problems. If they are stolen or lost, the card owner is responsible for reporting the loss to the credit card company. If the loss isn't reported immediately, the customer may have to pay for any charges made on the card. It is therefore very important for card holders to keep a list of all their credit card numbers in a convenient and reliable place.

Another problem is that many customers use their credit cards to purchase merchandise and services that they can't really afford. As a result, they have difficulty keeping up with their monthly payments. They have to pay high interest on the unpaid balance each month, and they go deeper and deeper into debt. Therefore, financial advisors suggest that consumers not have too many credit cards. They also advise consumers to try to pay the full amount of their credit card bills each month.

True or False?

1. Consumers like credit cards for their convenience.
2. All credit card owners must pay the total amount of their bills every month.
3. Credit card purchases can only be made in person.
4. People who order merchandise by telephone usually charge their purchases to their credit cards.
5. According to the reading, it's a good idea to have many different types of credit cards.

What's the Answer?

1. When you sign on the appropriate line, you _____.
    a. make an order
    b. fill out a form
    c. write your name *(circled)*

2. When you pay with interest, you pay _____.
    a. with a credit card
    b. a little bit more
    c. willingly

3. The balance on a monthly statement shows _____.
    a. the minimum payment
    b. the total amount the person has to pay
    c. the interest that has to be paid

4. If something happens unexpectedly, it happens _____.
    a. without warning
    b. soon
    c. right away

5. When people go into debt, it means they have _____.
    a. paid the full amount on their bills
    b. spent more money than they have
    c. gotten a cash advance from the bank

6. Unfortunately, people sometimes use credit cards _____.
    a. in shops and restaurants
    b. for shopping by mail or telephone
    c. more than they should

Survey

Take a survey of students in your class and other people you know. Ask people's opinions of using credit cards.

Do you use a credit card to pay for goods and services?
Which credit card do you prefer? Why?
In your opinion, what are the advantages of paying with a credit card?
What are the disadvantages?

Report your findings to the class and compare people's opinions.

CrossTalk

Have you ever misplaced or lost a credit card? What happened? Did anyone charge things to your credit card? What did you do? Talk with a partner and share your "misfortunes" with each other. Then tell the class about your experiences.

INTERCHANGE

Would You Be Interested in Applying for a P.J. Nickel's Charge Card?

A. Excuse me. Would you be interested in applying for a P.J. Nickel's charge card? We're offering a complimentary bottle of perfume today to everyone who applies.

B. Hmm. I suppose so.

A. All right. If you don't mind, I'd just like to get some information from you.

B. Okay.

A. What's your name?

B. George Parker.

A. And the address?

B. 1472 Central Avenue in Lakewood.

A. The zip code?

B. 09142.

A. And may I ask where you work?

B. Yes. I work at Precision Electronics.

A. Could you tell me what the telephone number is there?

B. 423-6333.

A. Do you have any major credit cards?

B. Yes. I have a MasterCard.

A. Would you happen to know your account number?

B. Hmm. Wait a minute. I think I have the card with me. Here it is. The number is 6157 9231 4820 2297.

A. And finally, would you tell me the name of your bank?

B. Yes. It's Lakewood Savings and Loan.

A. All right, Mr. Parker. Our credit department will review your application, and if it's approved, you should receive your P.J. Nickel's charge card within six weeks.

B. Okay.

A. And, Mr. Parker, please accept this bottle of perfume, compliments of P.J. Nickel's.

B. Thank you.

A. Excuse me. Would you be interested in applying for a _____ charge card? We're offering a complimentary _____ today to everyone who applies.

B. Hmm. I suppose so.

A. All right. If you don't mind, I'd just like to get some information from you.

B. Okay.

A. What's your name?

B. _____.

A. And the address?

B. _____ in _____.

A. The zip code?

B. _____.

A. And may I ask where you work?

B. Yes. I work at _____.

A. Could you tell me what the telephone number is there?

B. _____.

A. Do you have any major credit cards?

B. Yes. I have a _____.

A. Would you happen to know your account number?

B. Hmm. Wait a minute. I think I have the card with me. Here it is. The number is _____.

A. And finally, would you tell me the name of your bank?

B. Yes. It's _____.

A. All right, (Mr./Mrs./Ms./Miss) _____. Our credit department will review your application, and if it's approved, you should receive your _____ charge card within six weeks.

B. Okay.

A. And, (Mr./Mrs./Ms./Miss) _____, please accept this _____, compliments of _____.

B. Thank you.

A salesperson is signing you up for a department store charge card. Create an original conversation, using the model dialog above as a guide. Feel free to adapt and expand the model any way you wish.

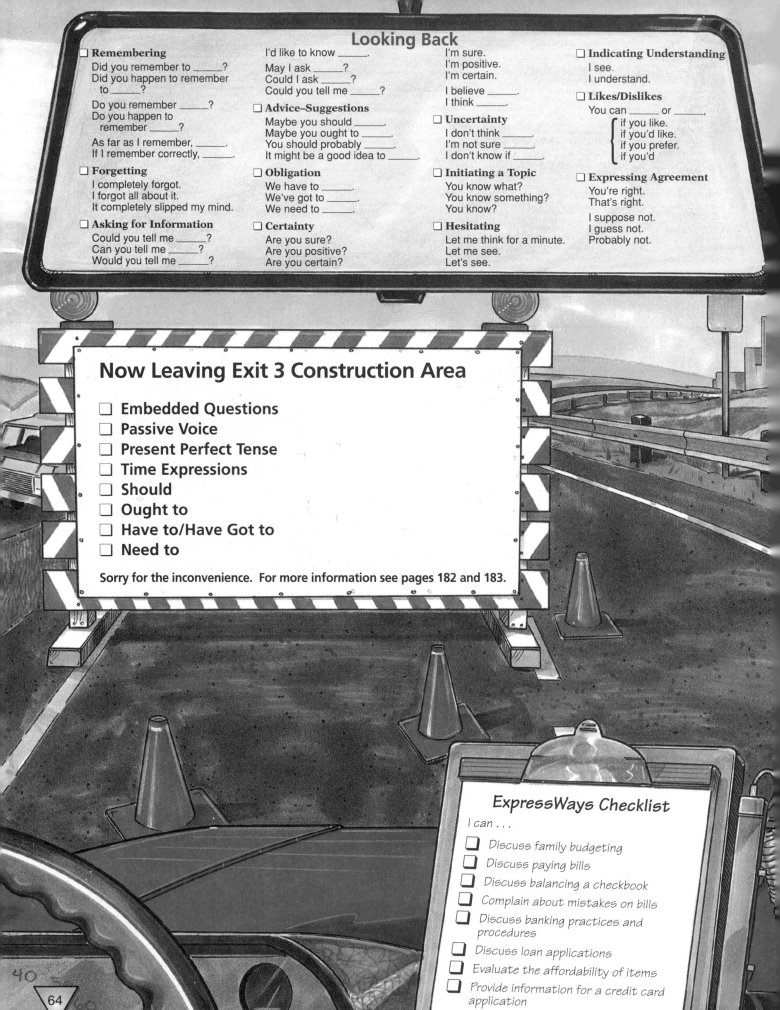

Looking Back

☐ Remembering
Did you remember to _____?
Did you happen to remember to _____?
Do you remember _____?
Do you happen to remember _____?
As far as I remember, _____.
If I remember correctly, _____.

☐ Forgetting
I completely forgot.
I forgot all about it.
It completely slipped my mind.

☐ Asking for Information
Could you tell me _____?
Can you tell me _____?
Would you tell me _____?

I'd like to know _____.
May I ask _____?
Could I ask _____?
Could you tell me _____?

☐ Advice–Suggestions
Maybe you should _____.
Maybe you ought to _____.
You should probably _____.
It might be a good idea to _____.

☐ Obligation
We have to _____.
We've got to _____.
We need to _____.

☐ Certainty
Are you sure?
Are you positive?
Are you certain?

I'm sure.
I'm positive.
I'm certain.
I believe _____.
I think _____.

☐ Uncertainty
I don't think _____.
I'm not sure _____.
I don't know if _____.

☐ Initiating a Topic
You know what?
You know something?
You know?

☐ Hesitating
Let me think for a minute.
Let me see.
Let's see.

☐ Indicating Understanding
I see.
I understand.

☐ Likes/Dislikes
You can _____ or _____,
{ if you like.
if you'd like.
if you prefer.
if you'd

☐ Expressing Agreement
You're right.
That's right.
I suppose not.
I guess not.
Probably not.

Now Leaving Exit 3 Construction Area

☐ **Embedded Questions**
☐ **Passive Voice**
☐ **Present Perfect Tense**
☐ **Time Expressions**
☐ **Should**
☐ **Ought to**
☐ **Have to/Have Got to**
☐ **Need to**

Sorry for the inconvenience. For more information see pages 182 and 183.

ExpressWays Checklist

I can . . .

☐ Discuss family budgeting
☐ Discuss paying bills
☐ Discuss balancing a checkbook
☐ Complain about mistakes on bills
☐ Discuss banking practices and procedures
☐ Discuss loan applications
☐ Evaluate the affordability of items
☐ Provide information for a credit card application

REST STOP

Take a break!

Have a conversation!

Here are some scenes from Exits 1, 2, and 3.

Who do you think these people are?
What do you think they're talking about?

In pairs or small groups, create conversations based on these scenes and act them out.

RULES AND REGULATIONS AT SCHOOL

Take Exit 4 to . . .

➤ Ask whether things are allowed, using impersonal expressions with *you*

➤ Tell people they aren't allowed to do things

➤ Understand traffic violations, using different verb tenses

➤ Understand traffic violations, using perfect modals

➤ Discuss parent-teacher communication, using reported speech, sequence of tenses, and embedded questions

➤ Discuss notes to a teacher, using reported speech

➤ Discuss student performance in school, using embedded questions

➤ Discuss grades and evaluation, using the passive voice, the past tense, and *should have*

Functions This Exit!

Permission
Requests
Asking for and Reporting
   Information
Possibility/Impossibility
Intention
Surprise–Disbelief
Attracting Attention

Janet is a passenger in Frank's car. Frank just did something he shouldn't have. What do you think Janet and Frank are saying to each other?

Mrs. Taylor is talking to her son about a telephone call she just received from her son's teacher. What do you think Mrs. Taylor and her son are saying to each other?

park

swim

A. Is parking permitted[1] here?
B. Yes, it is.[2]
A. Thanks.

A. Are people allowed to[3] swim here?
B. No, they aren't.[4]
A. Oh, okay. Thanks.

[1] Is ____ing allowed?
   Is it okay to ____?

[2] Yes, it is.   No, it isn't.
   Yes, it is.   No, it isn't.

[3] Are people permitted to ____?
   Are you allowed to ____?
   Are you permitted to ____?

[4] Yes, they are.   No, they aren't.
   Yes, you are.   No, you aren't.
   Yes, you are.   No, you aren't.

1 fish

2 take pictures

3 camp

4 roller skate

5 hitchhike

Ask if something is permitted.

ExpressWays

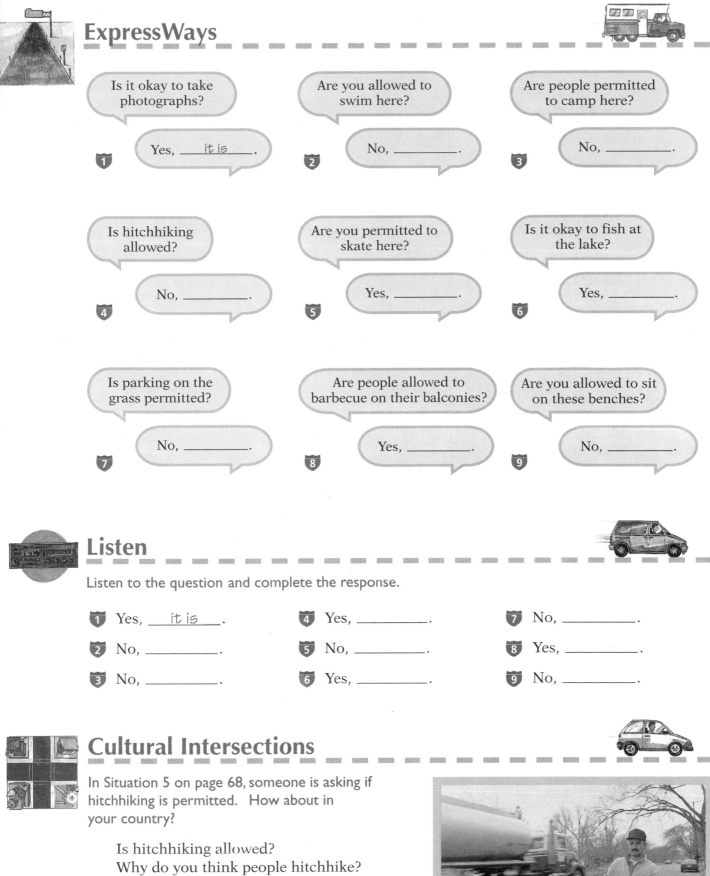

1. Is it okay to take photographs?
Yes, __it is__.

2. Are you allowed to swim here?
No, _____.

3. Are people permitted to camp here?
No, _____.

4. Is hitchhiking allowed?
No, _____.

5. Are you permitted to skate here?
Yes, _____.

6. Is it okay to fish at the lake?
Yes, _____.

7. Is parking on the grass permitted?
No, _____.

8. Are people allowed to barbecue on their balconies?
Yes, _____.

9. Are you allowed to sit on these benches?
No, _____.

Listen

Listen to the question and complete the response.

1. Yes, __it is__.
2. No, _____.
3. No, _____.
4. Yes, _____.
5. No, _____.
6. Yes, _____.
7. No, _____.
8. Yes, _____.
9. No, _____.

Cultural Intersections

In Situation 5 on page 68, someone is asking if hitchhiking is permitted. How about in your country?

Is hitchhiking allowed?
Why do you think people hitchhike?
What are the advantages of hitchhiking?
What are the dangers of hitchhiking (both for the hitchhiker and for the driver)?

A. Excuse me,[1] but **I don't think you're allowed to**[2] play ball in the park.

B. Oh?

A. Yes. There's a sign over there that says so.

B. Hmm. I guess I didn't notice it. Thanks for telling me.

A. You're welcome.

[1] Pardon me,

[2] I don't think you're permitted to
I don't think people are allowed to
I don't think people are permitted to

I don't think _____ing is allowed.
I don't think _____ing is permitted.

1

2

3

4

5

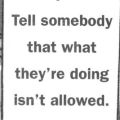

Tell somebody that what they're doing isn't allowed.

Fill It In!

Fill in the correct answer.

1 I don't think you're permitted _____ in this space.
   a. parking
   b. to park ✓

2 Are people allowed _____ their radios on the bus?
   a. playing
   b. to play

3 Excuse me. My son wants to know if _____ photographs is permitted.
   a. taking
   b. to take

4 I don't think _____ is allowed in this lake.
   a. to swim
   b. swimming

5 Is it okay _____ our bicycles in the park?
   a. riding
   b. to ride

6 Do you know if people are permitted _____ their dogs here?
   a. to walk
   b. walking

Listen

Listen and put the number under the correct sign.

_____   1   _____   _____   _____

Community Connections

Alone or with a partner, look for signs in your community—at bus stops, stores, libraries, parks, banks, post offices, or on buildings. Write down the location of the sign, what it says, and the purpose of the sign—to give instructions, to give information, or to tell about a restriction. For example:

Instructions: Bus: *Stand Behind the White Line*
                     Bank: *Wait for Next Available Teller*

Information: Department Store: *Store Hours 9-6*
                     Library: *Closed on Sunday*

Restrictions: Park: *Do Not Walk on the Grass*
                     Restaurant: *No Smoking*

Which student can find the most signs?
Who can find the most unusual sign?

A. Let me see your license.

B. Here you are, Officer. Tell me, what did I do wrong?

A. You went through a red light.

B. I did?

A. Yes, you did.

B. Oh. **I didn't realize that.**[1] **Would you possibly be willing to**[2] let me go with just a warning this time?

A. No. I'm afraid I can't. I'm going to have to give you a ticket.

B. Oh.

You went through a red light.

---

[1] I wasn't aware of that.

[2] Could you possibly
Could you please
Could I possibly ask you to

You were speeding.

1

Your inspection sticker has expired.

2

You made an illegal U-turn.

3

Your taillights aren't working.

4

You were going 75 in a 55-mile-per-hour zone.

5

You're a police officer! Give somebody a ticket!

ExpressWays

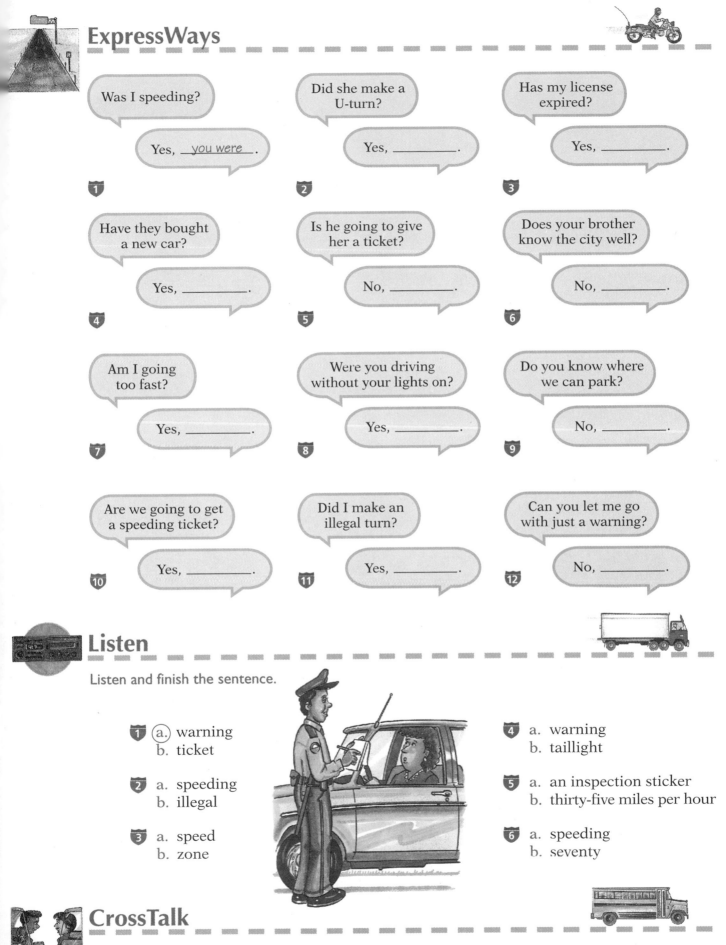

1. Was I speeding?
Yes, _you were_ .

2. Did she make a U-turn?
Yes, _____ .

3. Has my license expired?
Yes, _____ .

4. Have they bought a new car?
Yes, _____ .

5. Is he going to give her a ticket?
No, _____ .

6. Does your brother know the city well?
No, _____ .

7. Am I going too fast?
Yes, _____ .

8. Were you driving without your lights on?
Yes, _____ .

9. Do you know where we can park?
No, _____ .

10. Are we going to get a speeding ticket?
Yes, _____ .

11. Did I make an illegal turn?
Yes, _____ .

12. Can you let me go with just a warning?
No, _____ .

Listen

Listen and finish the sentence.

1.
a. warning
b. ticket

2.
a. speeding
b. illegal

3.
a. speed
b. zone

4.
a. warning
b. taillight

5.
a. an inspection sticker
b. thirty-five miles per hour

6.
a. speeding
b. seventy

CrossTalk

Have you ever been stopped by a police officer? What happened? Did you get a ticket?
Talk with a partner and then share your story with the class.

A. You know . . . I hate to be a "back-seat driver," but you really shouldn't have gone through that red light.

B. Oh?

A. Yes. You **could have**[1] gotten a ticket!

B. Hmm. You're right. I guess I just went through that red light without thinking. I must have had my mind on something else.

[1] might have

I can't believe he went through that red light!

get a ticket

I can't believe she made that U-turn!

1 be pulled over by a police officer

I can't believe he passed that car on the right-hand side!

2 cause an accident

I can't believe she cut in front of that big truck!

3 be hit

I can't believe he sped* through that school zone!

4 hit somebody

I can't believe she drove through that intersection so fast!

5 get us killed

You're a passenger in a car. The driver just did something he or she shouldn't have done.

* speed-sped-sped

Constructions Ahead!

I		
He		
She	should have	
It	could have	done that.
We	might have	
You	must have	
They		

1 You _____ forgotten your wife's birthday.
  (a.) shouldn't have
  b. should have

2 My goodness! She _____ gotten hurt!
  a. should have
  b. could have

3 That driver _____ hit those children!
  a. might have
  b. should have

4 I _____ gone to bed earlier last night. I'm exhausted today.
  a. should have
  b. shouldn't have

5 Why didn't Howard study for the test? He _____ gotten an A.
  a. shouldn't have
  b. could have

6 There aren't any cookies left. Someone _____ eaten them.
  a. should have
  b. must have

7 You _____ walked home alone at night in the dark. That was dangerous!
  a. might have
  b. shouldn't have

8 Roger came to work an hour late today. He _____ gotten up late.
  a. must have
  b. should have

9 I brought a map with me because I was afraid I _____ gotten lost.
  a. must have
  b. might have

10 I can't believe that guy cut in front of us! He _____ hit our car!
  a. could have
  b. must have

11 You look upset. Something terrible _____ happened.
  a. should have
  b. must have

12 Our teacher didn't come to class yesterday. She _____ been sick.
  a. should have
  b. might have

13 I'm sorry, Officer. I _____ gone through that red light.
  a. shouldn't have
  b. should have

14 Susan _____ been very happy. She got a big raise.
  a. should have
  b. could have

15 Careful! You _____ hit that tree!
  a. should have
  b. could have

16 We're exhausted. You _____ asked us so many questions.
  a. should have
  b. shouldn't have

REFLECTIONS
How do people drive in your area? Are they careful? Do they obey the "rules of the road"? Are there many accidents? What do you think causes most accidents? How can accidents be prevented?

Discuss in pairs or small groups, and then share your ideas with the class.

Fill It In!

Fill in the correct answer.

1 Should I ____ a U-turn?
    a. do
    b. make *(circled)*
    c. drive

2 Make a right at the next ____.
    a. intersection
    b. side
    c. zone

3 You just ____ a red light.
    a. passed
    b. went through
    c. sped

4 Harry was going fifty-five ____.
    a. speeding
    b. when he parked
    c. in a school zone

5 I'll try not to be a ____.
    a. police officer
    b. sticker
    c. "back-seat driver"

6 We could have ____.
    a. hit
    b. gotten hit
    c. caused

Listen

Listen and decide who is speaking.

1 a. driver *(circled)*
    b. police officer

2 a. driver
    b. police officer

3 a. passenger
    b. driver

4 a. passenger
    b. driver

5 a. driver
    b. police officer

6 a. driver
    b. "back-seat driver"

Community Connections

Tell about getting a driver's license where you live.

Where do you go to get a license?
How much does it cost?
Do you have to take a written test?
If so, what kinds of questions are there on the test?
Do you have to take a road test? Tell what happens during the road test.

CrossTalk

Talk with a partner about your experience getting a driver's license.

Were you nervous beforehand?
How was the written test?
What happened during the road test?

Compare with other students' experiences. (If you don't have a license, interview someone who does.)

Matching Lines

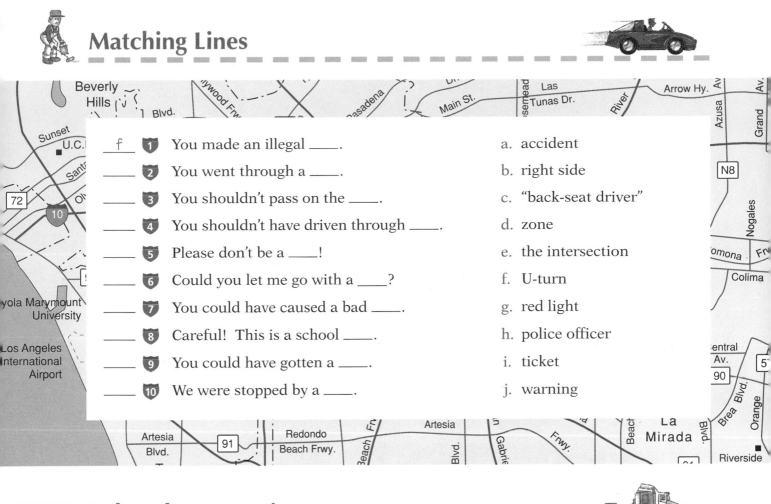

_f_	**1**	You made an illegal ____.	a. accident
____	**2**	You went through a ____.	b. right side
____	**3**	You shouldn't pass on the ____.	c. "back-seat driver"
____	**4**	You shouldn't have driven through ____.	d. zone
____	**5**	Please don't be a ____!	e. the intersection
____	**6**	Could you let me go with a ____?	f. U-turn
____	**7**	You could have caused a bad ____.	g. red light
____	**8**	Careful! This is a school ____.	h. police officer
____	**9**	You could have gotten a ____.	i. ticket
____	**10**	We were stopped by a ____.	j. warning

Cultural Intersections

Tell about speed limits in different places you have lived.

What is the speed limit on city streets?
What is the speed limit on highways?
How much is a ticket for speeding?
Do people drive the speed limit?
Do you think the speed limit is too slow
   or too fast?

InterActions

Oh, no! There's been an accident! Two cars have just hit each other.

What happened?
Is anyone hurt?
How badly are the cars
   damaged?
Are there any "eye
   witnesses"?
What happens when the
   police arrive?

With a group of students, create a
reenactment of the accident scene and present it to the class.

A. Johnny?

B. Yes?

A. Your teacher called today.

B. Really? What did she say?

A. She said you were doing poorly in social studies this marking period. **Is that true?**[1]

B. Yes, it is. **I was going to**[2] tell you, but I forgot.

[1] Is that right?
Is that so?

[2] I was planning to

Johnny is doing poorly in social studies this marking period.

your teacher

Betty is going to receive the "Outstanding Student" award this year.

1 your guidance counselor

Mark got into a fight in the lunchroom today.

2 the principal

Cathy has been late for school for the past several days.

3 your homeroom teacher

Jennifer needs to have her eyes checked.

4 the school nurse

Ted has to be examined by a physician before he can try out for the football team.

5 the football coach

Tell your child about a phone call you just got from school.

Constructions Ahead!

"Tim **is doing** well in school."
The teacher said Tim **was doing** well in school.

"You**'re going to get** an award on Friday."
The teacher said I **was going to get** an award on Friday.

"Sue **needs** help with her homework."
The teacher said Sue **needed** help with her homework.

"Bob and Bill **got** into a fight."
The teacher said Bob and Bill **had gotten** into a fight.

"You **haven't been studying** very hard."
The teacher said I **hadn't been studying** very hard.

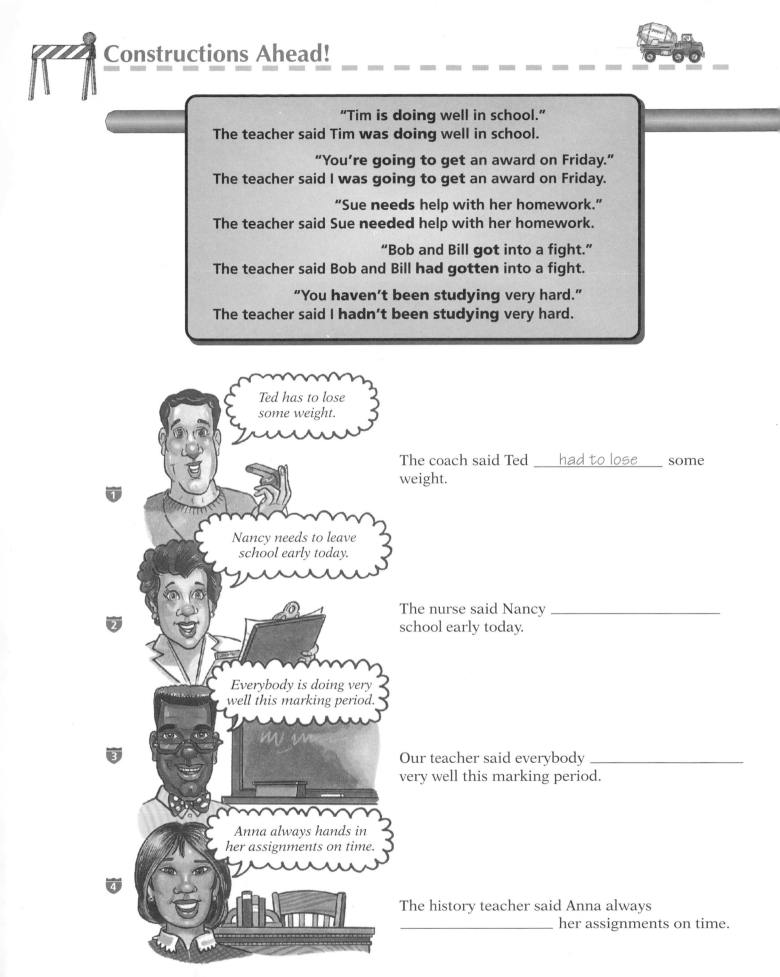

Ted has to lose some weight.

1 The coach said Ted ___had to lose___ some weight.

Nancy needs to leave school early today.

2 The nurse said Nancy _____ school early today.

Everybody is doing very well this marking period.

3 Our teacher said everybody _____ very well this marking period.

Anna always hands in her assignments on time.

4 The history teacher said Anna always _____ her assignments on time.

79

5. *He got into trouble at school today.*

Joey's mother said he _____ trouble at school today.

6. *You're going to get into a good college.*

The guidance counselor said I _____ a good college.

7. *I have to do my homework tonight.*

Brian said he _____ his homework tonight.

8. *You interrupt people in class all the time.*

The English teacher said I _____ people in class all the time.

9. *You forgot to answer five questions on the test.*

My math teacher said I _____ to answer five questions on the test.

10. *He's been coming late to school every day.*

Tommy's teacher said he _____ late to school every day.

11. *You're going to fail the test if you don't study.*

My science teacher said I _____ the test if I _____.

Cultural Intersections

In your country, how do parents and teachers communicate with each other?

Does the school ever call a student's home to talk to a parent?
If so, for what reasons?

Does a parent ever call the school?
If so, for what reasons?

Tell about any personal experiences you have had when someone from the school has called your home, or someone from your family has called the school.

CrossTalk

Talk with a partner about what it means to be a good English student. Do you agree or disagree with the following?

A good English student . . .

. . . *asks a lot of questions in class.*

. . . *writes down every new word in a notebook.*

. . . *speaks only English during class.*

. . . *never makes a mistake.*

. . . *listens very carefully to others.*

. . . *looks up every new word in the dictionary.*

. . . *memorizes lists of words.*

. . . *translates vocabulary words into his or her native language.*

Make a list of all the qualities you think a good English student should have. Then compare lists with other students in the class.

my gym teacher

my teacher

A. Could you please[1] write a note to my gym teacher?

B. To your gym teacher? Why? What do you want me to say?

A. Could you ask her to excuse me from gym today because I have a sore ankle?

B. All right.[2]

A. Thanks.

A. Could you please[1] write a note to my teacher?

B. To your teacher? Why? What do you want me to say?

A. Could you tell him I couldn't do my homework last night because I didn't feel well?

B. All right.[2]

A. Thanks.

[1] Could you possibly
Could I ask you to

[2] Okay.
Sure.

Dear Ms. Caruso,

Please let Susan skip glee club rehearsal today. She has laryngitis.

Sincerely,
Ms. Taylor

Dear Mr. Bridges,

Howard won't be able to help with the "Car Wash" this weekend. He has to attend his cousin's wedding.

Yours truly,
Albert Stone

Dear Mrs. Chen,

Please allow Carla to leave school an hour early today. She has a doctor's appointment.

Very truly yours,
Gloria Santa Cruz

1 the music teacher
2 the Drama Club advisor
3 Mrs. Chen

Dear Miss Day,

Please excuse Adam for being late for school yesterday. Our car wouldn't start.

Thank you,
Ann B. Larson

Dear Mr. Martinez,

Karen hasn't completed her science project yet. Our home computer erased her footnotes and bibliography.

Sincerely yours,
Mr. Potter

Ask your parent to write a note to school.

4 my homeroom teacher
5 my science teacher

Constructions Ahead!

Could you ask him to	{	allow me to leave early?
		let me skip the class picnic?
Could you tell her	{	I couldn't go to class because I was sick?
		I haven't completed my assignment yet?

1 Could you possibly ask him ____?
    (a.) to give me a hand
    b. he'll give me a hand.

2 Could you tell Mrs. Allen ____?
    a. I can't come to the school picnic
    b. let me come to the school picnic

3 Could you please tell her ____?
    a. can I help with the car wash
    b. I can help with the car wash

4 Could you ask those students ____?
    a. to be quiet
    b. I want them to be quiet

5 Could you please tell them ____?
    a. I'd like to talk to them
    b. to let me talk to them

6 Could you tell my science teacher ____?
    a. can I do the science project
    b. I couldn't do the science project

7 Could I ask you ____?
    a. to check your answers again
    b. you can check your answers

8 Could you please ask them ____?
    a. they can come to my office
    b. to come to my office

9 Could you please tell her ____?
    a. excuse me from my homework
    b. I couldn't do my homework

10 Could you ask the principal ____?
    a. to call me
    b. that I want to call her

11 Could you possibly ask her ____?
    a. to get here on time
    b. I'd like her to get here on time

12 Can you write a note and tell her ____?
    a. if I'm sick today
    b. I'm sick today

InterActions

You're a "parent." You have something very important to tell your child's teacher. Write a note to the teacher.

Another student in the class is your child's "teacher." Give your note to the "teacher." This person will write you back another note.

Everybody in the class should write two notes — a parent's note and a teacher's note.

A. Hello. I'm Mrs. Johnson.

B. Oh! You must be Lucy's mother!

A. Yes, I am. Nice to meet you.

B. Nice meeting you, too. Welcome to our "Open House" parents' night! **Do you have any questions you'd like to ask me?**[1]

A. Yes, as a matter of fact. **I was wondering**[2] whether you're pleased with Lucy's work so far this year.

B. Yes. She's one of the best students in the class.

---

[1] Do you have any questions for me?
Is there anything you'd like to ask me?

[2] I was wondering if you could tell me
I'd be interested to know
I'd be interested in knowing

Are you pleased with Lucy's work so far this year?

Yes. She's one of the best students in the class.

Mrs. Johnson

Are you satisfied with Eric's progress?

Yes. He's doing very nicely.

1 Mr. Winter

How is Flora getting along with the other children?

She's very friendly and outgoing.

2 Mrs. Santiago

Does Gary participate in class?

To be honest, he doesn't raise his hand as much as he could.

3 Henry Lewis

Why did Scott get a D for Conduct on his last report card?

To be honest with you, he often misbehaves during class.

4 Harriet Robbins

How is Melissa doing in math?

She's doing well with fractions, but she's having a little trouble with decimals.

5 Mr. and Mrs. Brooks

Greet your child's teacher at "Open House" parents' night.

Fill It In!

Fill in the correct answer.

1 I was wondering _____ with my son's progress.
    a. are you pleased
    b. if you're pleased
    c. whether are you pleased

2 I'd be interested in knowing _____.
    a. how my daughter is doing
    b. how is my daughter doing
    c. how's doing my daughter

3 I was wondering if you could tell me _____ with the other children.
    a. does Billy get along
    b. Billy gets along
    c. if Billy gets along

4 Excuse me. Could you possibly tell me _____?
    a. where's Room 200
    b. where it is Room 200
    c. where Room 200 is

5 Could I ask you _____ in class all the time or just occasionally?
    a. whether he misbehaves
    b. does he misbehave
    c. he misbehaves

6 I'd be interested to know _____ an A in math.
    a. why didn't Sally get
    b. why Sally didn't get
    c. why doesn't Sally get

7 I'd like to know _____ in the class.
    a. how many students there are
    b. how many are there students
    c. how many students are there

8 Would you tell me _____ with Robert's homework?
    a. if you're satisfied
    b. are you satisfied
    c. do you satisfy

Survey

Take a survey of students in your school and people in the community. Ask people's opinions of the role that parents should play in their children's schooling.

- Should parents check their children's homework?
- Should parents help children do their homework?
- Should parents limit the amount of time their children watch television?
- Should parents ask their children about their classes?
- How can parents help their children do well in school?
- Should parents speak with their children's teachers regularly?

Report your findings to the class. Compare the results of everybody's surveys.

I Just Received My Grades

A. I just received my grades.

B. How did you do?

A. Well, I got an A in history. I got a B plus (B+) in English. I received a B minus (B-) in calculus. And I got a C in biology.

B. Is that what you expected?

A. Well, not really. I knew I would get an A in history, and I was expecting to get a B plus in English. As far as calculus is concerned, I suppose I deserved a B minus. But I really don't think I should have gotten a C in biology.

B. Oh?

A. Yes. It seems to me I should have done better than that.

A. I just received the results of my performance evaluation.

B. How did you do?

A. Well, I was rated "Excellent" for Punctuality. I was rated "Good" for Efficiency. I was given a rating of "Fair" for Cooperation. And I was rated "Poor" for Attitude.

B. Is that what you expected?

A. Well, not really. I knew I would be rated "Excellent" for Punctuality, and I was expecting to be rated "Good" for Efficiency. As far as Cooperation is concerned, I suppose I deserved to be given a rating of "Fair." But I really don't think I should have been rated "Poor" for Attitude.

B. Oh?

A. Yes. It seems to me I should have done better than that.

Grades: A   A-   B+   B   B-   C+   C   C-   D   F

Performance Ratings: Excellent   Very Good   Good   Fair   Poor   Satisfactory   Unsatisfactory

---

You've just received an evaluation of your performance at work or at school. Discuss the results with a friend, using one of the model dialogs above as a guide. Feel free to adapt and expand the model any way you wish.

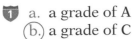 

Listen

Listen and decide what is being talked about.

1. a. a grade of A
   b. a grade of C *(circled)*

2. a. punctuality
   b. efficiency

3. a. school grades
   b. performance evaluation at work

4. a. punctuality
   b. cooperation

5. a. a grade of F
   b. a grade of B+

6. a. an evaluation of "Poor"
   b. an evaluation of "Excellent"

7. a. punctuality
   b. cooperation

8. a. attitude
   b. efficiency

Rate Yourself!

Rate yourself in the following areas. Try to be as "objective" as you possibly can. Use the performance ratings at the bottom of page 86 as a guide.

Punctuality	_____
Efficiency	_____
Cooperation	_____
Attitude	_____

Think about ways you might improve. Then rate yourself again at the end of your English course.

Cultural Intersections

Tell about schools in your country.

How many years do children go to school?
How old are children when they start?
How old are children when they finish?
Does everybody go to school?
Do all youngsters study the same things?
Do you think the school work is too difficult?
Do you think it's too easy?
Tell about the grading system.

Compare your country's schooling with other countries you know.

Years ago, children in rural areas attended one-room schoolhouses, where one teacher taught children of all ages and grade levels in one small classroom. The students were responsible for getting to school themselves. They arrived on foot, by bicycle, or even by horse. The school calendar revolved around the agricultural life of the community. School vacations were scheduled to allow children to work on their families' farms during the busy planting and harvesting times.

Of course, our education system now is quite different. The one-room schoolhouse has been replaced by large school complexes that contain many classrooms, long hallways, libraries, cafeterias, auditoriums, and gymnasiums. Many schools also have large playing fields for soccer, football, and baseball. Some even have swimming pools. Some students still walk or ride their bicycles to school, but nowadays, many arrive on school buses or in carpools. Some high school students even drive their own cars to school. Attendance until age sixteen is mandatory in most states. Many children in *extended day* programs stay in school until five or six o'clock because nobody is home to take care of them after school.

Recent developments in technology have also changed our educational system. One obvious influence on students today has been television. Young children start watching educational programs, such as *Sesame Street,* from the age of one or two. These programs are designed to entertain children while introducing them to numbers, letters, and simple math. For elementary and secondary students, there are after-school programs about math, science, and reading. Some universities offer credit for TV classes. Students can go to a classroom and watch a professor on television, or they can watch specially-designed programs at home.

Another big influence on education has been the personal computer, which is becoming an increasingly important educational tool. There are many software programs available on every school subject and topic and on many levels, from preschool to adult. Students enjoy using computers because they can work by themselves and at their own pace. Many software programs are designed as games. These programs are popular because they are entertaining and educational at the same time. In addition, many students use computers to get information from on-line services and the Internet, and many students use word-processing programs to do their assignments and papers.

The places where students learn and the tools they use have evolved as our society has evolved. But despite the advances of modern technology, education basically remains the student's responsibility.

True or False?

According to the reading, are the following statements true or false?

1. Society and technology influence educational changes.

2. Students under sixteen years of age must stay in school until their parents get home from work.

3. Studying in school complexes is better than studying in one-room schoolhouses.

4. Students always need a teacher to help them use their personal computers.

5. Watching television can be educational.

What's the Answer?

1. School *complexes* are _____.
   a. difficulties students have at school
   b. educational programs
   c. large buildings

2. *Agricultural life* refers to _____.
   a. life in other countries
   b. knowledge about different cultures
   c. life in farming communities

3. *Mandatory* attendance means _____.
   a. required
   b. recommended
   c. flexible

4. When something *evolves*, it _____.
   a. turns around
   b. changes
   c. involves a lot of people

5. When students work *at their own pace*, they _____.
   a. study at their own desks
   b. decide themselves how fast and how much to study
   c. find a quiet place to study

6. One-room schoolhouses were located _____.
   a. in agricultural areas
   b. in large complexes
   c. in urban areas

7. TVs and personal computers are examples of _____.
   a. places where students can learn
   b. modern technology
   c. software programs

8. It is possible for preschool children to _____.
   a. learn simple computer programs
   b. attend university classes
   c. get credit for watching specially-designed TV programs

9. More and more students are using _____ to do their assignments.
   a. schedules
   b. word-processing programs
   c. techniques

Your Turn

For Writing and Discussion

The reading on page 88 tells about changes that have taken place in U.S. schools. How about schools in your country?

How have schools changed over the past thirty years?
Do you approve of these changes or do you disapprove? Tell why.

Looking Back

Asking about Permissibility
Is _____ing permitted?
Is _____ing allowed?
Is it okay to _____?
Are people allowed to _____?
Are people permitted to _____?
Are you allowed to _____?
Are you permitted to _____?

Indicating Permissibility
Yes, _____ _____.
No, _____ _____.

I don't think you're allowed to _____.
I don't think you're permitted to _____.
I don't think people are allowed to _____.

I don't think people are permitted to _____.
I don't think _____ing is allowed.
I don't think _____ing is permitted.

Requests
Would you possibly be willing to _____?
Could you possibly _____?
Could you please _____?
Could I possibly ask you to _____?
Could I ask you to _____?

Responding to Requests
All right.
Okay.
Sure.

Asking for and Reporting Information
Is that true?
Is that right?
Is that so?

Do you have any questions you'd like to ask me?
Do you have any questions for me?
Is there anything you'd like to ask me?

I was wondering _____.
I was wondering if you could tell me _____.
I'd be interested to know _____.
I'd be interested in knowing _____.

Possibility
You could have _____ed.
You might have _____ed.

Intention
I was going to _____.
I was planning to _____.

Surprise–Disbelief
I didn't realize that.
I wasn't aware of that.

Attracting Attention
Excuse me.
Pardon me.

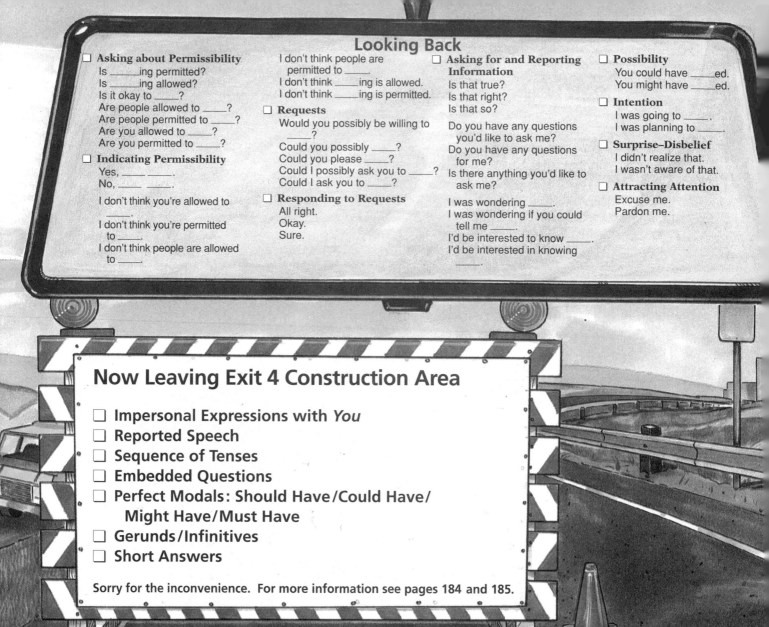

Now Leaving Exit 4 Construction Area

- ☐ Impersonal Expressions with *You*
- ☐ Reported Speech
- ☐ Sequence of Tenses
- ☐ Embedded Questions
- ☐ Perfect Modals: Should Have / Could Have / Might Have / Must Have
- ☐ Gerunds / Infinitives
- ☐ Short Answers

Sorry for the inconvenience. For more information see pages 184 and 185.

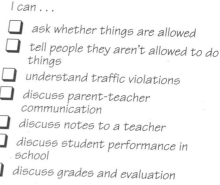

ExpressWays Checklist
I can . . .
- ☐ ask whether things are allowed
- ☐ tell people they aren't allowed to do things
- ☐ understand traffic violations
- ☐ discuss parent-teacher communication
- ☐ discuss notes to a teacher
- ☐ discuss student performance in school
- ☐ discuss grades and evaluation

90

Exit 5

AT WORK

Take Exit 5 to . . .

➤ Offer to help someone at work, using *want* + object + infinitive and *should have*

➤ Ask for feedback on job performance, using the present perfect tense

➤ Give feedback on job performance, using *could have, supposed to,* and short answers

➤ Correct someone at work

➤ Warn someone about a dangerous situation, using *had better*

➤ Make promises to fulfill responsibilities, using the present real conditional

➤ Offer suggestions at work, using *should* and *ought to*

Functions This Exit!

Offering to Do Something
Approval/Disapproval
Correcting
Warning
Advice–Suggestions
Promising
Asking for Repetition
Gratitude

Barry is asking his supervisor for feedback on something he has just done at work. What do you think Barry and his supervisor are saying to each other?

Doris is depending on her employee, Marta, to do something important at work. What do you think Doris and Marta are saying to each other?

A. Do you want me to[1] get that man's car?

B. That would be great. Are you sure you don't mind?

A. No, not at all. **I'd be happy to.[2]**

B. I really appreciate it. I should have gotten it a little while ago, but I've been so busy I haven't had a chance.

A. Don't worry. I'll take care of it.

B. Thanks.

---

[1] Would you like me to

[2] I'd be glad to.

get that man's car

1 take the mail to the post office

2 sweep* up the sawdust around your bench

3 write out next week's work schedule

4 do a printout of last month's sales figures

5 ring* the church bells

Offer to help somebody at work.

* sweep-swept-swept
  ring-rang-rung

Constructions Ahead!

I want $\begin{Bmatrix} \text{you} \\ \text{him} \\ \text{her} \\ \text{them} \end{Bmatrix}$ to carry the bags.   He wants $\begin{Bmatrix} \text{me} \\ \text{us} \end{Bmatrix}$ to carry the bags.

1 Do you want me to write out tomorrow's work schedule?

No. ___I want you to write out___ the schedule for the rest of the week.

2 Do you want Carol to give out the mail now?

No. _____ the paychecks.

3 Does Mr. Taylor want me to sweep out the dining room now?

No. _____ the kitchen first.

4 Does your mother want you and your brother to do the dishes?

No. _____ our homework.

5 Do you want your employees to work until 5:30 tonight?

No. _____ until 8:00.

6 Do you want the waiter to bring the check?

No. _____ dessert.

Listen

Listen and decide where the conversation is taking place.

1
 (a.) an office
 b. a restaurant
 c. a post office

3
 a. a cafeteria
 b. a movie theater
 c. a factory

5
 a. a doctor's office
 b. a restaurant
 c. a health club

2
 a. a stockroom
 b. a department store
 c. an airport

4
 a. an office
 b. an employee lounge
 c. a parking lot

6
 a. a factory
 b. an expressway
 c. a parking lot

CrossTalk

I've been so busy I haven't had a chance to write to my grandparents. I think I'll write them a letter tonight.

I've been working so hard I haven't had time to clean my house. I think I'll clean it this Saturday.

I've been so tired at night I haven't had the energy to pay my bills. I guess I'll pay them this weekend.

We all have things that for some reason we "haven't had a chance to do." Talk with a partner. Tell what these things are, tell why you haven't done them, and then tell about your plans for doing them.

A. Did I write up this invoice all right?

B. Yes. You wrote it up very well.

A. I just wanted to be sure. I haven't written up very many invoices since I started here.

B. Well, you did **an excellent job!**[1]

A. Thanks.

[1] a very good job
a fine job

write up this invoice

1 repair the muffler

2 set* up this display

3 gift-wrap this box

4 make this Caesar salad

5 press this wedding gown

Ask your supervisor for feedback on your work.

* set-set-set

Fill It In!

Fill in the correct answer.

1 I _____ a muffler in a long time.
   a. didn't repair
   b. repaired
   c. haven't repaired _(circled)_

2 Monica _____ the meeting room a long time ago.
   a. set up
   b. has set up
   c. sets up

3 I think _____ that invoice the day before yesterday.
   a. I wrote up
   b. I've written up
   c. I'll write up

4 _____ since I started working here.
   a. I was late
   b. I've never been late
   c. I didn't be

5 I _____ a Caesar salad in a long time.
   a. didn't make
   b. haven't made
   c. made

6 I can't believe it! Our new mechanic says _____ an engine before!
   a. he repaired
   b. he'll repair
   c. he hasn't repaired

7 The truth is I still _____ last night's homework assignment.
   a. have done
   b. do
   c. haven't done

8 I'm sorry. _____ to press your suit.
   a. I forget
   b. I forgot
   c. I haven't forgotten

Listen

Listen and decide where the conversation is taking place.

1
   a. a library
   b. a theater
   c. an airport _(circled)_

2
   a. a restaurant
   b. a factory
   c. a supermarket

3
   a. a post office
   b. a department store
   c. a factory

4
   a. a supermarket
   b. the Personnel Office
   c. a bank

5
   a. a service station
   b. a grocery store
   c. a restaurant

6
   a. a parking lot
   b. an assembly line
   c. a shopping mall

CrossTalk

You did an excellent job!

You did a very good job!

You did a fine job!

These are the words an employee likes to hear from a boss or supervisor! Talk with a partner: Why do you think it's important to give people "positive feedback" at work? Make a list of reasons. Then compare lists with other students and discuss your ideas.

A. Do you approve of the way[1] I hooked up this computer?

B. Well . . . To be honest with you,[2] I think you could have hooked it up a little better.

A. Oh, I see. I'll try to do better next time.

[1] What do you think of the way
How do you like the way

[2] To be perfectly honest with you,
In all honesty,

hook up this computer

1 assemble this circuit board

2 draw* these blueprints

3 arrange the furniture

4 hang* the wallpaper

5 give that injection

Ask if your supervisor approves of something you did.

* draw-drew-drawn
hang-hung-hung

Fill It In!

FIll in the correct answer.

1 You ____ job.
   a. made a fine
   b. did an excellent *(circled)*
   c. done a good

2 ____ of the way I arranged the room?
   a. How do you like
   b. How do you think
   c. Do you approve

3 In all ____, you could have done a better job.
   a. honest with you
   b. honesty
   c. perfectly honest

4 I just wanted ____.
   a. to be sure
   b. check
   c. all right

5 How do you like ____?
   a. of the way I fixed it
   b. the way I fixed it all right
   c. the way I fixed it

6 ____ you think of the way Gary arranged the furniture?
   a. How much
   b. Which do
   c. What do

ExpressWays

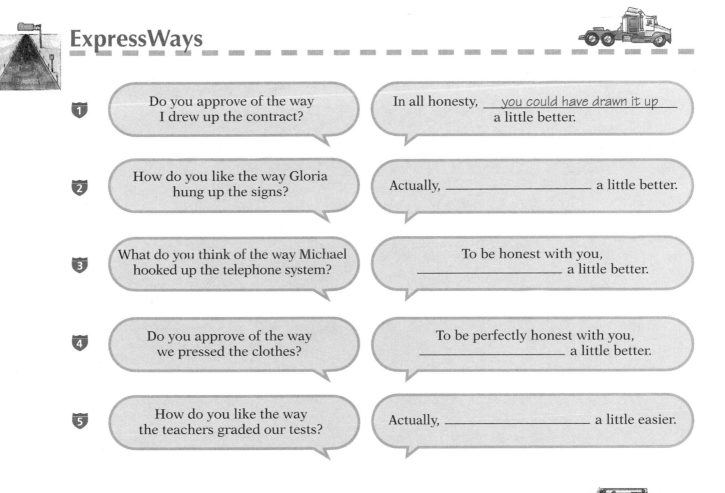

1 Do you approve of the way I drew up the contract?

In all honesty, __you could have drawn it up__ a little better.

2 How do you like the way Gloria hung up the signs?

Actually, _____ a little better.

3 What do you think of the way Michael hooked up the telephone system?

To be honest with you, _____ a little better.

4 Do you approve of the way we pressed the clothes?

To be perfectly honest with you, _____ a little better.

5 How do you like the way the teachers graded our tests?

Actually, _____ a little easier.

InterActions

Imagine that the people on page 96 all try to do their work better the next time. Now they're all asking, "How did I do THIS time?" What do you think will happen next? With a partner, choose one of the situations and continue the scene any way you wish. Present your role play to the class. Compare how the different situations get resolved.

A. Henry?
B. Yes?
A. You aren't frying the eggs **the right way.**[1]
B. I'm not?
A. No. You're supposed to grease the pan first.
B. I am?
A. Yes, you are.
B. Oh. **I didn't know that.**[2] **Thanks for telling me.**[3]

[1] right
correctly

[2] I wasn't aware of that.

[3] Thank you for telling me.
Thanks for letting me know.
Thank you for letting me know.

You're supposed to grease the pan first.

Henry doesn't know how to fry the eggs.

The arrows on the boxes have to point up.

1 Vincent doesn't know how to stack the boxes.

The label should be on the top of the can, not on the side.

2 Beverly doesn't know how to label the canned goods.

The item number goes in the left column.

3 Alan doesn't know how to enter the data.

You need to use some adhesive when you make the connections.

4 John doesn't know how to connect the pipes.

You're jumping when you're supposed to kick.

5 Terry doesn't know how to do the dance routine.

Correct an employee about something he or she is doing wrong.

Matching Lines

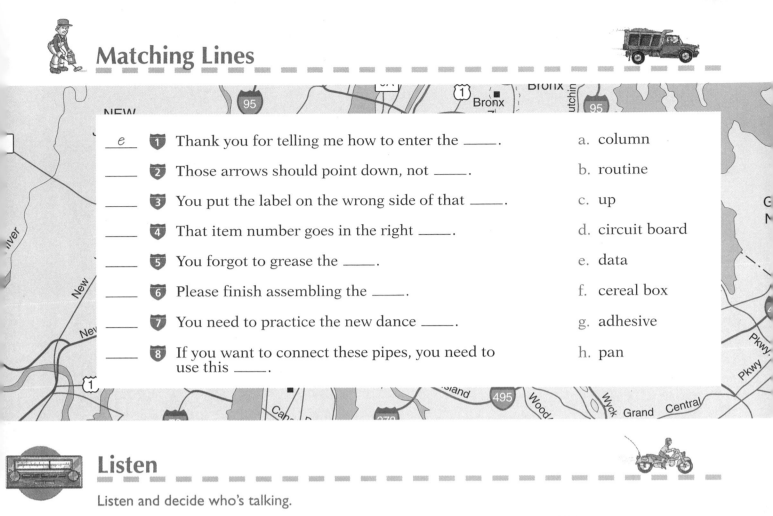

_e_ **1** Thank you for telling me how to enter the ____.

____ **2** Those arrows should point down, not ____.

____ **3** You put the label on the wrong side of that ____.

____ **4** That item number goes in the right ____.

____ **5** You forgot to grease the ____.

____ **6** Please finish assembling the ____.

____ **7** You need to practice the new dance ____.

____ **8** If you want to connect these pipes, you need to use this ____.

a. column

b. routine

c. up

d. circuit board

e. data

f. cereal box

g. adhesive

h. pan

Listen

Listen and decide who's talking.

1 a. a cook
   b. a waiter
   (c.) an accountant

2 a. a mail carrier
   b. a repairperson
   c. a librarian

3 a. a security guard
   b. an auto mechanic
   c. a computer programmer

4 a. a gardener
   b. a plumber
   c. a carpenter

5 a. a secretary
   b. a chef
   c. a bellhop

6 a. a cashier
   b. a teacher
   c. a nurse

CrossTalk

Tell about a time YOU made a mistake at work.

What happened?
Did anyone notice?
What did you do?
What did your employer say?
Did your co-workers say anything?
How did you feel?
What did you say?

Share your experience with a partner and then tell the class about it.

REFLECTIONS
Are you able to "take criticism?" How do you react when someone criticizes you? Why do you think the ability to take criticism is important on the job?

Discuss in pairs or small groups, and then share your ideas with the class.

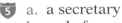

99

A. The sale ends on Saturday.

B. Excuse me, Mrs. Williams, but **that isn't exactly right.**[1]

A. Oh?

B. Yes, **ma'am.**[2] Actually, the sale ends on FRIDAY.

A. Oh. **Thank you for calling that to my attention.**[3]

---

[1] that isn't quite right
that isn't exactly correct
that isn't quite correct
that really isn't so

[2] ma'am [*for a woman*]
sir [*for a man*]

[3] Thank you for correcting me.

The sale ends on Saturday.

on FRIDAY

Mrs. Williams

The magazines go in Aisle Three.

Aisle TWO

1 Ms. Gardner

You're scheduled to receive your next raise in October.

in JULY

2 Mr. Grinchly

Our next shipment will go out on the twenty-third.

on the twenty-SIXTH

3 Mr. Benson

According to your file, you've accumulated ten days of leave time.

TWELVE days

4 Miss Pratt

Ladies and gentlemen, the correct time here in New York is four o'clock.

FIVE o'clock

5 Captain Kirk

Politely correct your boss or supervisor.

Listen

Listen to each conversation and answer the questions.

Conversation 1

1. Where does this conversation take place?
   a. in a factory
   b. in a grocery store
   c. in a department store

2. What is the person looking for?
   a. tofu
   b. Frozen Foods
   c. Charlie

Conversation 2

3. What is the relationship between these two people?
   a. father and son
   b. bookkeeper and employee
   c. two roommates

4. How does he spell his name?
   a. Kraft
   b. Crast
   c. Craft

Conversation 3

5. Where does this conversation take place?
   a. in an office
   b. in a kitchen
   c. in a restaurant

6. What is the problem?
   a. Bill doesn't feel well.
   b. There's a mistake on the bill.
   c. He doesn't have enough money.

Conversation 4

7. Where does this conversation take place?
   a. at an airport
   b. in a cafeteria
   c. in a classroom

8. What is the relationship between these two people?
   a. two friends
   b. boss and secretary
   c. teacher and student

CrossTalk

Have you ever corrected your boss, your supervisor, or your teacher about anything? Why did you correct the person? What did the person say? Were you embarrassed? Talk with a partner, and then tell the class about your experience.

Figure It Out!

Write down ten "facts." Some of them should be true, and others should be false. Can other students find the "false facts" and correct them?

Tokyo is the capital of Japan.

There are five continents.

Yes. That's right.

Actually, there are SEVEN continents.

Watch your step!

The floor is slippery.

fall

A. Be careful![1]

B. Excuse me?[2]

A. You'd better watch your step!

B. Oh?

A. Yes. The floor is slippery. You might fall.

B. Thanks for warning me.[3]

Don't block the doorway!

It's an emergency entrance.

get in the way

A. Be careful![1]

B. Excuse me?[2]

A. You'd better not block the doorway!

B. Oh?

A. Yes. It's an emergency entrance. You might get in the way.

B. Thanks for warning me.[3]

---

[1] Careful!
Look out!
Watch out!

[2] Pardon me?
[*less formal*]
Huh?

[3] Thanks for the warning.

Put on your helmet!

This is a hard-hat area.

1 get hit by a falling object

Don't tamper with that fuse box!

It's very high voltage.

2 get a bad shock

Watch your fingers!

The conveyor belt moves quickly.

3 hurt yourself

Wear your protective clothing!

This is a radioactive area.

4 get contaminated

Don't disturb the lion!

She's ferocious.

5 get hurt

Warn somebody about something!

Constructions Ahead!

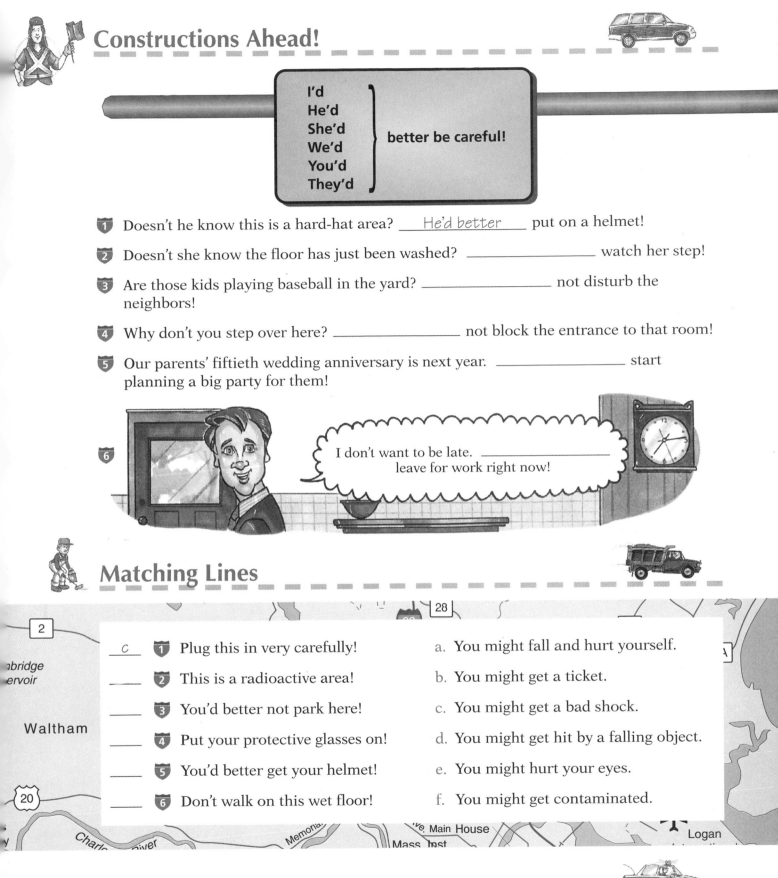

> I'd
> He'd
> She'd
> We'd
> You'd
> They'd
> } **better be careful!**

1 Doesn't he know this is a hard-hat area? ___He'd better___ put on a helmet!

2 Doesn't she know the floor has just been washed? _____ watch her step!

3 Are those kids playing baseball in the yard? _____ not disturb the neighbors!

4 Why don't you step over here? _____ not block the entrance to that room!

5 Our parents' fiftieth wedding anniversary is next year. _____ start planning a big party for them!

6 I don't want to be late. _____ leave for work right now!

Matching Lines

_c_	**1** Plug this in very carefully!		a.	You might fall and hurt yourself.
___	**2** This is a radioactive area!		b.	You might get a ticket.
___	**3** You'd better not park here!		c.	You might get a bad shock.
___	**4** Put your protective glasses on!		d.	You might get hit by a falling object.
___	**5** You'd better get your helmet!		e.	You might hurt your eyes.
___	**6** Don't walk on this wet floor!		f.	You might get contaminated.

Your Turn

For Writing and Discussion

Make a list of safety procedures that could help prevent injuries at work or at school. Present your list to the class, and compare everybody's suggestions.

A. Marvin? Can I **depend on**[1] you to deposit this money in the bank before it closes?

B. Yes. **Absolutely!**[2]

A. It's really important. If you don't, all the checks we wrote today will bounce.

B. Don't worry. I promise I'll deposit it. You can **depend on**[1] me.

A. Thanks.

[1] rely on
count on

[2] Definitely!

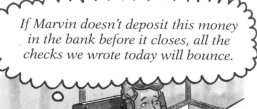

> If Marvin doesn't deposit this money in the bank before it closes, all the checks we wrote today will bounce.

> If Harold doesn't turn on the burglar alarm before he leaves, we might get robbed.

1

> If Gloria doesn't turn off the air conditioner before she leaves for the weekend, the motor could burn out.

2

> If Bob doesn't have these glasses cleaned by 4:30, we won't be ready for the late-afternoon crowd.

3

> If Ms. Jones doesn't get this report in the mail by five o'clock, we might lose our government contract.

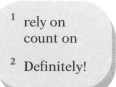

4

> If Jane doesn't give the people from "Tooth-Brite Toothpaste" a first-class presentation, we may not get their business.

5

Ask an employee to do something important.

Constructions Ahead!

> If
> { I, we, you, they } don't
> { he, she, it } doesn't
> arrive soon, the meeting will be canceled.

1 Michael had better leave soon. If ___*he doesn't leave soon*___, he might miss his flight!

2 We should deposit our paychecks right away. If _____, the checks we wrote last week will bounce!

3 Alice had better get to work on time today! If _____, she could lose her job! She's been late every day this week!

4 Do you know where I live? If _____, I can give you directions.

5 Howard, slow down! If _____, you'll get a speeding ticket!

6 I hope I get paid tomorrow. If _____, I might have to ask you to lend me some money.

7 Look at those kids up in that tree! They'd better be careful! If _____, they might fall.

8 I hope it snows tonight. If _____, school will be open tomorrow, and I'll have to take the biology test!

Your Turn

For Writing and Discussion

Complete the following any way you wish and compare with other students' "conclusions."

If I miss my next English class, ...

If I don't do my homework this weekend, ...

If I go to sleep after midnight tonight, ...

If I don't eat breakfast tomorrow morning, ...

If I learn to speak English well, ...

105

INTERCHANGE

I Was Wondering If I Might Possibly Offer a Suggestion

A. Excuse me, Mrs. Baskin.

B. Yes?

A. I was wondering if I might possibly offer a suggestion.[1]

B. Of course.[2]

A. Well, I've been thinking about this for a while . . .

B. Yes?

A. I think we should[3] pipe music into the work areas as a way of increasing employee morale and productivity.

B. Hmm. That's an interesting suggestion. I'll give it some serious consideration.

---

[1] [*less direct*]
Could I possibly offer a suggestion?
May I possibly offer a suggestion?

[*direct*]
I have a suggestion.
I'd like to offer a suggestion.

[2] Sure.
By all means.

[3] I think we ought to
I suggest that we
It seems to me that we should

A. Excuse me, _____.

B. Yes?

A. I was wondering if I might possibly offer a suggestion.[1]

B. Of course.[2]

A. Well, I've been thinking about this for a while . . .

B. Yes?

A. I think we should[3] _____.

B. Hmm. That's an interesting suggestion. I'll give it some serious consideration.

Make a suggestion to your employer, using the model dialog above as a guide. Feel free to adapt and expand the model any way you wish.

Fill It In!

Fill in the correct answer.

1 I'll _____ some thought.
- **a.** give it
- b. make it
- c. do it

2 I was wondering _____.
- a. may I offer a suggestion
- b. I might offer a suggestion
- c. if I might offer a suggestion

3 I'd like _____.
- a. have a suggestion
- b. to offer a suggestion
- c. to do a suggestion

4 _____ to me that we should talk.
- a. I think
- b. I suggest
- c. It seems

5 I think _____ to be careful.
- a. you should
- b. you ought
- c. you're

6 Could I possibly offer _____?
- a. a consideration
- b. a suggestion
- c. a question

7 I suggest that _____.
- a. we have a meeting
- b. we will have a meeting
- c. we had a meeting

8 _____ a suggestion.
- a. I'd give
- b. I have
- c. I make

9 I promise I'll _____.
- a. thinking about it
- b. by all means
- c. think about it

10 I'll give your suggestion some _____.
- a. suggestion
- b. consideration
- c. decision

Cultural Intersections

In some countries, it is common for employees to offer suggestions for improving efficiency or working conditions. They sometimes do this by speaking with their bosses or supervisors. Or they might put their ideas in writing and leave them in "suggestion boxes" at work.

Does this ever happen in your country? How do employees offer suggestions on the job?

InterActions

Set up a suggestion box in your classroom! Write one or two suggestions for changing things in your English classroom. Read everybody's suggestions. As a class, vote on the suggestions you think are the best.

Before the efforts of the labor movement in the United States in the twentieth century, working conditions in factories, mines, and many other workplaces were very bad. Small children worked in factories instead of going to school. These children worked long hours and were paid very low wages. In many workplaces, they weren't allowed to take breaks, eat, or even go to the bathroom. Many workers were immigrants with little knowledge of English. Even those who could speak English didn't question their employers' decisions because they were afraid of losing their jobs.

Factories were overcrowded and unsafe. Factory machinery was dangerous, and the long workday made employees tired. Also, many workers were injured in accidents.

It took a great tragedy to make the country realize that working conditions were so bad. In 1911, a fire broke out in the Triangle Clothing Factory in New York City. The doors of the factory had been locked in order to keep the workers at their machines, so it was impossible for most of them to escape. Many people lost their lives in the fire.

After the fire, many organizations called for improvements in working conditions. Child labor laws ended the use of young children as a workforce, and other new laws required employees to pay their workers a minimum hourly wage set by the government. In addition, employees who worked more than forty hours a week had to be paid overtime. Eventually, a Social Security system was established to provide a minimum monthly payment to retired workers.

In 1971, the Department of Labor established the Occupational Safety and Health Administration (OSHA). This agency sets standards for workplace safety. The agency is

supposed to inspect workplaces to make sure employers are following safety regulations, especially in industries with potential safety hazards, such as chemical manufacturing, factories with dangerous machinery, and workplaces where employees might be exposed to radiation.

The labor movement has helped provide workers in the United States with better and safer working conditions. However, many people feel that not enough has been done, and labor organizations continue to work hard to see that these goals are met.

What's the Meaning?

1. Factories were *overcrowded*.
   a. dirty
   b. too large
   c. filled with too many people ✓

2. Workers were given very *low wages*.
   a. little money
   b. few jobs
   c. few hours

3. Some workers were *immigrants* with little knowledge of English.
   a. excellent workers
   b. people without money
   c. people who came from other countries

4. A *great tragedy* caused people to improve working conditions.
   a. wonderful thing
   b. terrible event
   c. good situation

5. OSHA sets safety *standards*.
   a. schedules
   b. inspections
   c. requirements

6. OSHA looks for potential *safety hazards*.
   a. powerful security systems
   b. dangerous conditions
   c. experts

What's the Answer?

1. The minimum wage law _____.
   a. required children to stay in school until a minimum age
   b. provided a minimum payment to retired workers
   c. set a minimum hourly wage ✓

2. OSHA is an agency that _____.
   a. ended the use of children in the workplace
   b. requires employers to pay a minimum wage
   c. enforces federal standards

3. According to the reading, OSHA probably _____.
   a. inspects chemical factories
   b. inspects labor organizations
   c. makes sure employers pay minimum wage

4. According to the reading, working conditions in the United States _____.
   a. are perfect
   b. can still be improved
   c. are worse than ever

Your Turn

For Writing and Discussion

Tell about working conditions in your country.

Are there child labor laws?

Is there a minimum wage for workers?

Does the government provide money for workers after their retirement?

What standards are there for workplace safcty?

Do government agencies regulate working conditions?

What do they do?

Looking Back

☐ **Offering to Do Something**

Do you want me to ____?
Would you like me to ____?

I'd be happy to.
I'd be glad to.

☐ **Asking for Approval**

Did I ____ all right?
Do you approve of the way
   I ____ed?
What do you think of the
   way I ____ed?
How do you like the way I ____ed?

☐ **Expressing Approval**

You did an excellent job!
You did a very good job!
You did a fine job!

☐ **Expressing Disapproval**

To be honest with you, . . .
To be perfectly honest with you, . . .
In all honesty, . . .

☐ **Correcting**

You aren't ____ing the right way.
You aren't ____ing right.
You aren't ____ing correctly.

That isn't exactly right.
That isn't quite right.
That isn't exactly correct.
That isn't quite correct.
That really isn't so.

☐ **Responding to Correction**

I didn't know that.
I wasn't aware of that.

Thanks for telling me.
Thank you for telling me.
Thanks for letting me know.
Thank you for letting me know.
Thank you for calling that to
   my attention.
Thank you for correcting me.

☐ **Warning**

Be careful!
Careful!
Look out!
Watch out!

☐ **Offering a Suggestion**

[*least direct*]
I was wondering if I might
   possibly offer a suggestion.

[*less direct*]
Could I possibly offer a
   suggestion?
May I possibly offer a
   suggestion?

[*direct*]
I have a suggestion.
I'd like to offer a suggestion.

I think we should ____.
I think we ought to ____.
I suggest that we ____.
It seems to me that we should
   ____.

Now Leaving Exit 5 Construction Area

☐ **Want + Object + Infinitive**
☐ **Present Real Conditional**
☐ **Should Have**
☐ **Could Have**
☐ **Present Perfect Tense**
☐ **Had Better**
☐ **Short Answers**
☐ **Supposed to**

Sorry for the inconvenience. For more information see pages 186 and 187.

ExpressWays Checklist

I can . . .

☐ Offer to help someone at work
☐ Ask for and give feedback on job performance
☐ Correct someone
☐ Warn someone about a dangerous situation
☐ Make promises to fulfill responsibilities
☐ Offer suggestions at work

40
110
60
70

Exit 6

RIGHTS AND RESPONSIBILITIES

Take Exit 6 to . . .

➔ Express dissatisfaction with products, using short answers

➔ Express dissatisfaction with services, using different verb tenses

➔ Make requests of neighbors, using short answers and sequence of tenses

➔ Discuss housing repair problems, using reported speech and sequence of tenses

➔ Complain about housing problems, using the present perfect tense

➔ Discuss employee rights

➔ Discuss taking legal action

➔ Discuss citizens' rights

Functions This Exit!
Complaining
Satisfaction/Dissatisfaction
Advice–Suggestions
Focusing Attention
Preference
Requests
Asking for and Reporting
   Information
Asking for and Reporting
   Additional Information
Want–Desire
Apologizing
Intention
Certainty
Disappointment

Henry is returning something to a store because there's a problem with it. What do you think Henry and the salesperson are saying to each other?

Greg is talking to Stella about a problem he's having in his apartment building. What do you think Greg and Stella are saying to each other?

A. May I help you?

B. Yes. I'd like to return this garden hose I bought here last week.

A. **What's the problem with it?**[1]

B. It leaks.

A. It does?

B. Yes, it does.

A. Oh, I'm sorry. **Would you like**[2] a refund?

B. Actually, **I'd prefer to**[3] exchange this one for one that doesn't leak.

A. Certainly. Sorry for the inconvenience.

[1] What seems to be the problem with it?
What seems to be the matter with it?

[2] Do you want
Would you care for

[3] I'd rather

It leaks.

garden hose

It won't work on my computer.

1 software program

It's too difficult for me to put together.

2 model airplane kit

It's been opened.

3 bottle of aspirin

It doesn't whistle.

4 teapot

It can't get "Radio Moscow."

5 shortwave radio

There's a problem with something you bought. Return it to the store.

Fill It In!

Fill in the correct answer.

1 Sorry for the ____.
  a. refund
  b. exchange
  c. inconvenience

2 What's the ____ with it?
  a. wrong
  b. matter
  c. exchange

3 ____ to have a refund.
  a. I'd prefer
  b. I'd apologize
  c. I'd rather

4 ____ some advice?
  a. Do you like
  b. Would you like
  c. Would you care about

5 ____ for a larger size?
  a. Would you like
  b. Would you care
  c. Do you think

6 I'd like to ____ this pan.
  a. exchange
  b. refund
  c. care for

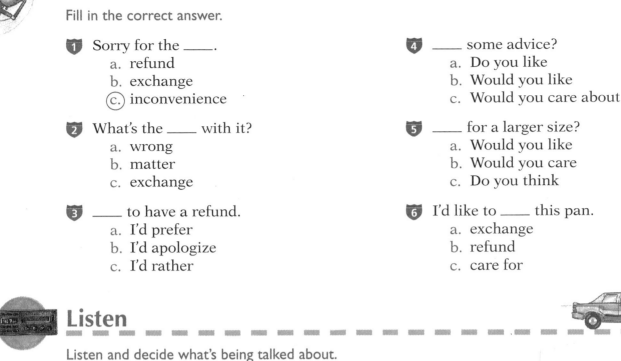

Listen

Listen and decide what's being talked about.

1 a. a puzzle
  b. a TV
  c. a teapot

2 a. a door
  b. a bottle of medicine
  c. an automobile

3 a. money
  b. a salesperson
  c. a teapot

4 a. a personal computer
  b. a cup of coffee
  c. a bottle of aspirin

5 a. a bottle of soda
  b. a refrigerator
  c. a television set

6 a. dollar bills
  b. boots
  c. vitamins

CrossTalk

Have you ever bought something that didn't work?
Talk with a partner about your experience.

What did you buy?
What was the problem?
What did you do? Did you fix it?
  Did you exchange it?
What did the store do about the problem?

Share your experiences with the class.

Cultural Intersections

Do stores in your country exchange items? What happens when you buy something that you are dissatisfied with?

A. May I help you?

B. Yes. I had this toaster fixed here last week, but it still isn't working right.

A. Oh. What's **the problem**[1] with it?

B. It's still burning the toast. And now, **in addition to that,**[2] it sparks when I plug it in.

A. I see. How long has it been sparking?

B. Since I had it fixed here last week.

A. **I apologize for**[3] the inconvenience. We'll try to fix it again for you.

B. Thank you.

> [1] the matter
> wrong
>
> [2] besides that
> on top of that
>
> [3] I'm sorry for

It's still burning the toast. It sparks when I plug it in.

this toaster

It's still stalling all the time. The oil is leaking.

1 my car

It's still running fast. The alarm doesn't work.

2 this digital watch

It still doesn't get Channel 9. It doesn't get Channel 7.

3 this TV set

The tape still doesn't rewind. The volume control isn't working.

4 this cassette player

The paper is still ripping. The "P" and "G" keys are sticking.

5 this portable typewriter

You had something fixed at the store where you bought it, but it still isn't working right! Take it back to the store.

What's the Word?

A. I (have) _____had_____¹ my laptop computer (repair) _____² here a few days ago, but it still isn't (work) _____³ correctly.

B. What's the matter with it?

A. The keys are still (stick) _____⁴. And now, every time I turn it on, the picture on the screen (move) _____⁵ up and down. It's (do) _____⁶ that since I (get) _____⁷ it fixed here a few days ago.

B. I'm really sorry. We'll try to (fix) _____⁸ it correctly next time.

Listen

Listen to the complaint and decide what's being talked about.

1
  a. a bicycle
  b. a watch
  c. a dog

2
  a. a software program
  b. a puzzle
  c. a cassette player

3
  a. an automobile
  b. an umbrella
  c. the gardener

4
  a. a bus
  b. a garden hose
  c. a coffeemaker

5
  a. a car
  b. a typewriter
  c. a door

6
  a. a photograph
  b. a textbook
  c. a TV set

7
  a. a model airplane kit
  b. a chocolate cake
  c. a portable computer

8
  a. a microwave oven
  b. a fireplace
  c. a sink

9
  a. a salesperson
  b. a table
  c. a computer

InterActions

The people on page 114 went back to the stores, picked up the items, brought them home, and tried them again. But believe it or not ... they still weren't working! The stores hadn't fixed them properly! So each of these people took the items back to the stores and complained again.

With a partner, choose one of the situations on page 114 and continue the conversation at the store. Present your role plays to the class. Compare how each situation gets resolved.

Could You Please Turn Down the Volume on Your TV?

A. Could you please[1] turn down the volume on your TV?

B. Turn down the volume?

A. Yes . . . if you wouldn't mind.[2] I don't mean to complain, but[3] you're keeping all the neighbors up.

B. I am?

A. Yes, you are.

B. Oh! I had no idea[4] I was keeping all the neighbors up. I'm sorry.[5]

A. That's okay.

---

[1] Could you possibly
Could I possibly ask you to

[2] if you don't mind
if it's not too much trouble

[3] I don't want to complain, but
I hate to complain, but

[4] I didn't realize
I didn't know

[5] I apologize.
Please accept my apology.
Please forgive me.

Your neighbor is doing something that you're upset about. Complain to your neighbor about it.

Constructions Ahead!

"You're disturbing the neighbors!"

I didn't know
I didn't realize
I had no idea
} I was disturbing the neighbors.

Your bicycle is blocking the entrance!

I didn't realize *my bicycle was blocking the entrance*

1

Water is coming into our apartment!

I had no idea
_____
_____
_____

2

Your dogs are eating our flowers!

I didn't know
_____
_____
_____

3

Your stereo is keeping us up!

I didn't realize
_____
_____
_____

4

Your children are playing in our yard!

I had no idea
_____
_____
_____

5

The rent is late!

I didn't realize
_____
_____
_____

6

CrossTalk

Talk with a partner about your relationship with your neighbors.

Is it easy or difficult to get along with your neighbors?
Have you ever had a problem with one of your neighbors?
If so, what was the problem?
Did you talk to your neighbor about it?
What happened?

Tell the class about your discussion.

A. I'm really **annoyed with**[1] the superintendent.

B. Why?[2]

A. Several days ago I told him our toilet wouldn't flush, and I asked him if he could fix it.

B. And what did he say?

A. He said he would get to it right away, but he hasn't done it yet.

B. Have you spoken to him again?

A. No, not yet. **I'm planning to**[3] speak to him later today.

B. You really should.

Our toilet won't flush. Can you fix it?

I'll get to it right away.

the superintendent

---

[1] upset with
[stronger]
mad at
angry at

[2] How come?

[3] I'm going to
I intend to

We don't have any heat in our living room. Would you please take care of it?

I'll have it checked immediately.

1 the landlord

Our apartment is crawling with cockroaches. Can you call an exterminator?

I'll have your apartment sprayed in a day or so.

2 the building manager

You're late refunding our security deposit. Could you please return it right away?

I'll put it in the mail by Saturday.

3 my former landlord

Some people are bringing pets into the building. What should we do about it?

I'll call a meeting of the members of the association.

4 the head of the condo association

Our bushes look terrible. Can you trim them?

I'll take care of them immediately.

5 the gardener

You're really annoyed about a housing problem you're having. Tell a friend about it.

Constructions Ahead!

> "Our stove **is** broken."
> I told him our stove **was** broken.
>
> "We **don't have** any heat."
> I told her we **didn't have** any heat.
>
> "Our refrigerator **won't work**."
> I told him our refrigerator **wouldn't work**.
>
> "We **can't pay** the rent."
> I told her we **couldn't pay** the rent.

1 "The parking lot looks terrible."   I told him ___the parking lot looked terrible___.

2 "My radiator won't work."   I told her _____.

3 "We don't have electricity."   I told the landlord _____.

4 "Our dishwasher is broken."   I told Mrs. Williams _____.

5 "I'll mail the security deposit today."   I told them _____.

6 "The washer and dryer aren't working."   I told Mr. Lee _____.

7 "I can't close my front door."   I told the superintendent _____.

8 "I want to move out of the building."   I told the landlord _____.

More Constructions Ahead!

> "**Are** you **going to fix** the door?"
> I asked him if he **was going to fix** the door.
>
> "**Did** you **call** the plumber?"
> I asked her if she **had called** the plumber.
>
> "**Can** you **repair** the stove?"
> I asked him if he **could repair** the stove.
>
> "**Would** you **take care of** the heat?"
> I asked her if she **would take care of** the heat.

1 "Can you fix the elevator?"   I asked him ___if he could fix the elevator___.

2 "Would you call an exterminator?"   I asked Mrs. Baxter _____.

3 "Will you return our security deposit?"   I asked them _____.

4 "Did the mail arrive?"   I asked my neighbor _____.

5 "Should we move our car?"   I asked her _____.

6 "Is the building going to be sold?"   I asked the landlord _____.

7 "Can you repair the front stairs?"   I asked the superintendent _____.

8 "Have you called an exterminator?"   I asked him _____.

ExpressWays

Complete the conversation. Then practice it with a partner.

> *The radiator in our bedroom needs to be fixed.*
>
> *The light switch in the kitchen is broken.*
>
> *Can you repair the front steps?*
>
> *Can you look at the leak in our living room ceiling?*

> *I'll look at it tomorrow morning.*
>
> *I'll send an electrician as soon as possible.*
>
> *I'll take care of it by the end of the week.*
>
> *I can't fix it myself, but I'll call someone to take care of it.*

A. I saw the superintendent this morning.

B. Oh. Did you tell him about the radiator in our bedroom?

A. Yes. I told him _____ the radiator in our bedroom needed to be fixed _____¹.

B. And what did he say?

A. He said _____²·

B. And did you tell him about the light switch in the kitchen?

A. Yes. I told him _____³·

B. And what did he say?

A. He said _____⁴·

B. And did you ask him about the front steps?

A. Yes. I asked him _____⁵·

B. And what did he say?

A. He said _____⁶·

B. And did you ask him about the ceiling in our living room?

A. Yes. I asked him _____⁷·

B. And what did he say?

A. He said _____⁸·

B. Do you think he'll fix everything?

A. He said he would.

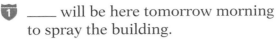

Fill It In!

Fill in the correct answer.

1. ____ will be here tomorrow morning to spray the building.
    a. An exterminator
    b. A sprinkler
    c. A plumber

2. I'll have the bushes ____ next weekend.
    a. crawling
    b. flushed
    c. trimmed

3. We don't have ____ our bedroom.
    a. heat in
    b. a deposit on
    c. pets into

4. There are ____ all over our kitchen!
    a. bushes
    b. crawling
    c. cockroaches

5. Our toilet is broken. It won't ____.
    a. crush
    b. brush
    c. flush

6. I'll take care of everything ____.
    a. immediately
    b. away
    c. a week or so

7. The landlord said he didn't want to ____ our security deposit.
    a. spray
    b. return
    c. check

8. He's the new ____ manager.
    a. building
    b. neighbor
    c. former

9. The ____ association is meeting tonight.
    a. meeting
    b. condo
    c. inconvenience

10. I'm ____ with our upstairs neighbors.
    a. trouble
    b. upset
    c. mad

11. I'm ____ meet with them tomorrow.
    a. intend to
    b. going
    c. planning to

12. I'm really mad at ____.
    a. our security deposit
    b. our kitchen ceiling
    c. our superintendent

InterView

Interview a classmate. Take notes, and then report to the class about your interview.

Have you ever had problems with your apartment?

What were they?

Did you talk to the landlord or superintendent about them?

What did he or she say?

Did he or she fix things?

How long did it take?

Was the work done well?

How did you contact the landlord?

Was it easy or difficult?

A. Hello. This is Mrs. Peters in Apartment 5.

B. Yes? What can I do for you?

A. I'm calling to find out why you haven't gotten rid of the mice in our apartment yet.

B. Well, Mrs. Peters, I've been very busy.

A. You know, **I'm a little disappointed.**[1] You really should have gotten rid of them by now.

B. You have to understand. These things take time.

A. Well, **to tell the truth,**[2] **I'd rather not**[3] have to call the Health Department. Do you think you might be able to take care of it?

B. Of course. I'll do it right away.

get rid of the mice in our apartment

call the Health Department

Mrs. Peters in Apartment 5

[1] [*stronger*]
I'm very disappointed.

[2] to be honest with you
honestly

[3] I'd prefer not to

repair the hot water heater

call the Housing Authority

1 Mr. Oyola in Apartment 3B

give a lease to us

refer this to a lawyer

2 Barbara Thomas from your building on Center Street

return our security deposit

take this to Small Claims Court

3 Rick Simpson, who lived in Building 3C

remove the lead paint in the hallway

call City Hall

4 Mrs. Chen on the third floor

turn on the heat

contact the media

5 Mr. Goldin at 345 Main Street

Call about a housing problem you're having, and threaten to take further action.

Fill It In!

Fill in the correct answer.

1 I'm calling to find out ____.
    (a.) why you haven't fixed our dishwasher
    b. why haven't you fixed our dishwasher
    c. have you fixed our dishwasher

2 I'd like to know ____.
    a. will you return our security deposit
    b. when you'll return our security deposit
    c. when you return our security deposit

3 Please tell me ____.
    a. where is the exterminator
    b. where's the exterminator
    c. where the exterminator is

4 I'd like to know ____.
    a. when are you going to move
    b. when you going to move
    c. when you're going to move

5 I'm calling to find out ____.
    a. why you didn't turn on the heat
    b. you turned on the heat
    c. why did you turn the heat on

6 I'd like to know ____.
    a. how long have you had cockroaches
    b. you've had cockroaches how long
    c. how long you've had cockroaches

InterActions

These people are still upset!

Mrs. Peters still has mice in her apartment. Mr. Oyola's hot water heater hasn't been repaired yet. Barbara Thomas hasn't been given a lease. Rick Simpson's security deposit hasn't been returned. There's still lead paint in Mrs. Chen's hallway. And the heat still hasn't been turned on in Mr. Goldin's apartment. What are these people going to do? Who are they going to call? With a partner, choose a situation, decide on the person's course of action, create a role play, and present it to the class.

Community Connections

Find the names, addresses, and telephone numbers of agencies or organizations in your community that offer assistance to people with housing problems, such as those on page 122. Call one of these agencies, find out the kinds of problems they handle, and ask how people can file a complaint. Report your findings to the class.

A. I'm really **annoyed with**[1] the foreman.

B. Why?

A. He's **insisting that I**[2] skip all my breaks.

B. He can't do that! Breaks are guaranteed in our contract.

A. Are you **sure?**[3]

B. **Absolutely!**[4] You should tell him that.

A. I couldn't. I'm afraid he'd fire me!

B. Oh, come on! He can't fire you for that.

A. Are you **sure?**[3]

B. **Absolutely!**[4]

[1] upset with [stronger] mad at angry at	[2] requiring me to [stronger] forcing me to making me	[3] positive certain	[4] Definitely! Positively!

Skip all your breaks!

the foreman

Breaks are guaranteed in our contract.

Work on Labor Day!

the boss

1 It's a legal holiday.

Work overtime for no extra pay!

the manager

2 You're supposed to receive time-and-a-half for overtime.

Come back to work right after you have the baby!

my supervisor

3 You're entitled to maternity leave.

Help move the scenery!

the director

4 It's against union regulations.

Do your trapeze act without a net!

the new owner of the circus

5 It's against the safety rules.

Tell a friend that what that person's boss is doing is illegal.

Fill It In!

Fill in the correct answer.

1 The boss is ____ me work this weekend.
   a. firing
   (b.) making
   c. requiring

2 I'm not sure, but I think the manager is ____ at me.
   a. certain
   b. angry
   c. forcing

3 Are you ____ about that?
   a. positively
   b. sure
   c. insisting

4 Yes. ____!
   a. Absolutely
   b. Positive
   c. Certain

5 ____ are guaranteed.
   a. Overtime pay
   b. Breaks
   c. Legal holiday

6 Why is your supervisor ____ at you?
   a. requiring
   b. certain
   c. mad

7 Our manager is ____ that we work tonight.
   a. making
   b. insisting
   c. forcing

8 They can't ____ you to do that job!
   a. force
   b. insist
   c. make

9 I was ____ with my supervisor today.
   a. annoying
   b. upset
   c. positively

10 That's against ____.
   a. time-and-a-half
   b. maternity leave
   c. safety regulations

Listen

Listen and decide which rule is being broken.

> ____ Workers are required to wear helmets at all times!
>
> ____ Maternity leave is guaranteed.
>
> _1_ Employees are not required to work on legal holidays.
>
> ____ All workers are entitled to one morning and one afternoon break.
>
> ____ Employees are entitled to time-and-a-half pay for overtime work.

Cultural Intersections

Tell about workers' rights in your country.

Are there laws and regulations that protect the rights of workers?
What are some of these laws and regulations?
Are there organizations that can help with employment problems?
What do these organizations do?

A. You seem upset. Is anything **the matter?**[1]

B. Yes, as a matter of fact. My former landlord absolutely refuses to return my security deposit.

A. Well, can I offer you some advice?

B. Sure. What?

A. **I think you should**[2] hire a lawyer.

B. Hmm. I hadn't thought of that. That's a good idea.

---

[1] wrong
troubling you

[2] I think you ought to
I suggest that you
I'd suggest that you
It seems to me you should
If I were you, I'd

> My former landlord absolutely refuses to return my security deposit.

hire a lawyer

> The painters who ruined our new carpet refuse to pay for the damages.

1 sue them

> The used car dealer who just sold me this "lemon" refuses to fix it.

2 call the Better Business Bureau

> I think my neighbors across the hall are abusing their children.

3 call the police

> Even though I've complained about it, I'm continually being overcharged on my electric bills.

4 call the Mayor's Office of Consumer Affairs

> The gossip columnists are printing lies about my personal life and destroying my movie career.

5 take them to court

Give advice to a friend who is troubled about something.

Fill It In!

Fill in the correct answer.

1 It seems to me you should _____.
   a. call the police
   b. calling the police

2 _____ you sue them.
   a. You ought to
   b. I'd suggest that

3 You seem upset about something. What's _____ you?
   a. wrong
   b. troubling

4 If I were you, _____ them to court.
   a. I'd take
   b. I'd suggest

5 I'd really rather not _____ a lawyer.
   a. hiring
   b. hire

6 My lawyer thinks I ought to _____ the Better Business Bureau.
   a. contact
   b. take

Can You Help These People?

These people are upset and need some advice. What do you suggest? Compare your ideas with other students' suggestions.

1 *My landlord refuses to fix the radiator in my apartment!*

2 *My next-door neighbors keep leaving their garbage in the hallway!*

3 *My boss is forcing me to work overtime this weekend!*

4 *The bank says two of my checks have bounced, but I don't believe it!*

5 *The phone company has charged me for several long-distance calls I didn't make!*

6 *An intersection near our house is very dangerous. We need a traffic light there!*

7 *A factory is dumping oil and wastes into a small stream near our house!*

8 *Our rent has been raised four times in the last year!*

9 *It snowed three days ago, and the roads still haven't been cleared!*

You Should Write to the Mayor and Express Your Opinion

A. You know . . . **If you ask me,**[1] they're building too many offices and apartment buildings in our neighborhood.

B. **What makes you say that?**[2]

A. The area is becoming noisy and crowded, and traffic during rush hour is terrible.

B. Hmm. You seem to feel very strongly about that.

A. I do.

B. In that case, why don't you write to the mayor?*

A. Write to the mayor?

B. Yes. You should write to the mayor and express your opinion.

A. That's a good idea. Thanks for the suggestion.

[1] In my opinion, As far as I'm concerned,	[2] Why do you say that? Why? How come?

*__Some forms of citizen participation__
  write to/call the president
  write to/call our congressman/congresswoman/senator
  write to/call the governor/mayor/city manager
  ask to speak at a town meeting
  send a letter to the editor of the newspaper
  call one of the radio talk shows

A. You know . . . If you ask me,[1] _____.

B. What makes you say that?[2]

A. _____.

B. Hmm. You seem to feel very strongly about that.

A. I do.

B. In that case, why don't you _____?*

A. _____?

B. Yes. You should _____ and express your opinion.

A. That's a good idea. Thanks for the suggestion.

You're talking with a friend about a local, national, or international issue. Create an original conversation, using the model dialog above as a guide. Feel free to adapt and expand the model any way you wish.

Your Turn

For Writing and Discussion

Write a letter to a newspaper about an issue you feel strongly about. It may be a local, national, or international issue. Have your teacher collect everybody's letters and "publish" them for the class to read and react to.

Match the Expressions

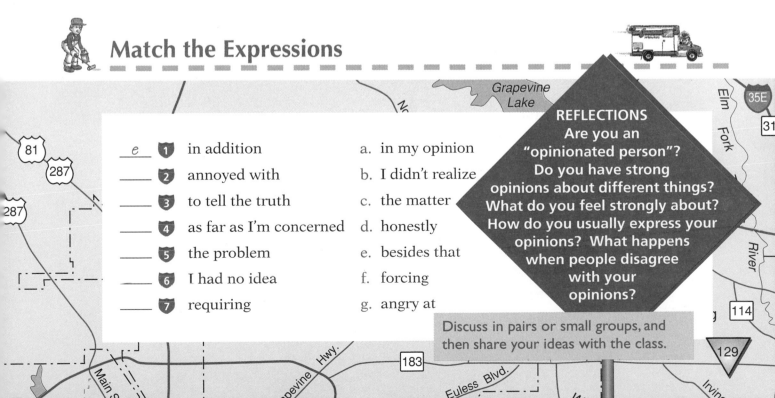

_e_ **1** in addition	a. in my opinion
___ **2** annoyed with	b. I didn't realize
___ **3** to tell the truth	c. the matter
___ **4** as far as I'm concerned	d. honestly
___ **5** the problem	e. besides that
___ **6** I had no idea	f. forcing
___ **7** requiring	g. angry at

REFLECTIONS
Are you an "opinionated person"? Do you have strong opinions about different things? What do you feel strongly about? How do you usually express your opinions? What happens when people disagree with your opinions?

Discuss in pairs or small groups, and then share your ideas with the class.

Citizens in the United States have many opportunities to participate in the political life of their communities and the nation. They participate by voting, by expressing their views to elected officials, and by voicing their opinions in newspapers and on radio and television.

The most obvious way citizens participate is by voting. They vote for their political representatives at the local, state, and national levels. At the local level, citizens vote to elect the officials who govern their communities, such as the mayor and members of the city council. Citizens also vote for state government officials, such as the governor and their district representatives to the state legislature. At the national level, citizens vote for members of the House of Representatives and the Senate and, of course, for the president of the United States.

In addition to electing officials, citizens sometimes have the opportunity to vote on referenda. A referendum is a proposal on a specific issue, such as raising local taxes, building new schools, establishing a state lottery, or banning smoking in public places. The proposal appears on the election ballot, and the voters approve or reject it by voting *Yes* or *No*.

Another way citizens participate in government is by communicating with elected officials. They write letters; send faxes, telegrams, and e-mail (electronic mail); and make telephone calls to offices of their local, state, and national representatives. They can also express an opinion in a petition — a written statement requesting a change in a law or policy. They collect a large number of signatures of people who support this view, and then send the petition to the appropriate representative.

Citizens also make their opinions known through the media. They write letters to local newspapers and other publications. These letters are often published in a special *Letters to the Editor* section. There are also many radio *talk shows* that allow the audience to voice their opinions on the air. These shows usually have a host who interviews special guests about an important issue. After the interview, the host takes calls from listeners who wish to ask questions, argue about the issue, or just offer an opinion. Many popular TV shows offer the same opportunity. The host discusses a topic with one or more special guests and then invites the studio audience to participate. On some programs, viewers at home are also invited to call the TV station and take part in the discussion.

The right to vote is a key benefit of a democratic system. Unfortunately, many citizens don't take advantage of their right. Fewer than fifty percent of all eligible voters have participated in recent national elections. Many citizen groups, such as the League of Women Voters, work hard to encourage voters to participate, so that more and more citizens will exercise this important privilege.

True or False?

1. There are many ways that U.S. citizens can take part in their government.
2. Unfortunately, U.S. citizens are not allowed to vote for local officials.
3. Some television and radio stations offer opportunities for citizen participation.
4. Most U.S. citizens vote in national elections.
5. U.S. citizens are required to vote in local, state, and national elections.

What's the Meaning?

1. Citizens can express their *views* to their representatives.
   - a. panoramas
   - (b.) opinions
   - c. sights

2. Some people would like to *ban* smoking in public places.
   - a. allow
   - b. consider
   - c. stop

3. There are many *opportunities* for citizen participation.
   - a. chances
   - b. volunteers
   - c. suggestions

4. Citizens can also make their opinions known through the *media*.
   - a. newspapers
   - b. radio and newspapers
   - c. radio, television, and newspapers

5. Many groups hope more citizens will *exercise* the right to vote.
   - a. remember
   - b. use
   - c. approve

6. Unfortunately, many *eligible* voters haven't voted recently.
   - a. qualified
   - b. elected
   - c. desirable

Cultural Intersections

Tell about the political system of your country.

What officials do people vote for at the local and national level?
Are there ever any *referenda* on important issues?
Is it common for citizens to write to their local or national representatives?
Do people write to newspapers and express their views?
Are there radio or television talk programs where people call in to express their opinions?
What percent of citizens usually vote in your country's elections?

InterActions

As a class, create a TV talk program! Decide on a host, the special guests, and the "hot issue" to be discussed on today's program. The rest of the class is the studio audience. Members of the audience should ask a lot of questions and express their opinions. If possible, videotape your program and play it back.

131

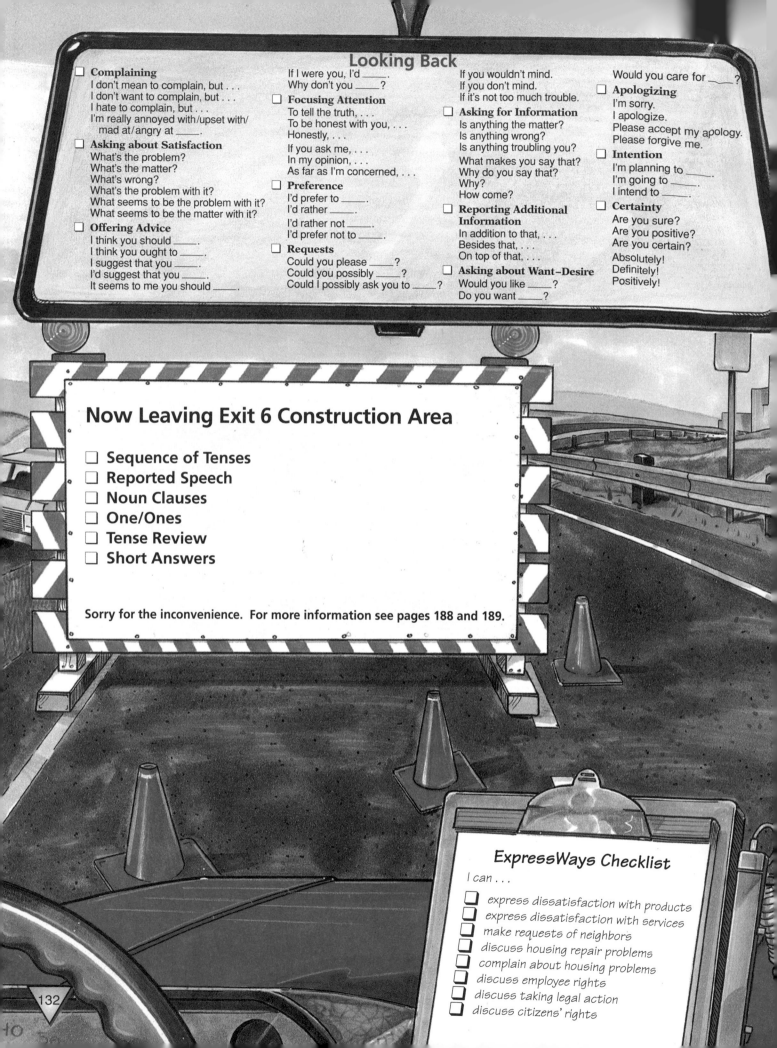

Looking Back

Complaining
I don't mean to complain, but . . .
I don't want to complain, but . . .
I hate to complain, but . . .
I'm really annoyed with/upset with/
  mad at/angry at _____.

Asking about Satisfaction
What's the problem?
What's the matter?
What's wrong?
What's the problem with it?
What seems to be the problem with it?
What seems to be the matter with it?

Offering Advice
I think you should _____.
I think you ought to _____.
I suggest that you _____.
I'd suggest that you _____.
It seems to me you should _____.

If I were you, I'd _____.
Why don't you _____?

Focusing Attention
To tell the truth, . . .
To be honest with you, . . .
Honestly, . . .

If you ask me, . . .
In my opinion, . . .
As far as I'm concerned, . . .

Preference
I'd prefer to _____.
I'd rather _____.

I'd rather not _____.
I'd prefer not to _____.

Requests
Could you please _____?
Could you possibly _____?
Could I possibly ask you to _____?

If you wouldn't mind.
If you don't mind.
If it's not too much trouble.

Asking for Information
Is anything the matter?
Is anything wrong?
Is anything troubling you?

What makes you say that?
Why do you say that?
Why?
How come?

Reporting Additional Information
In addition to that, . . .
Besides that, . . .
On top of that, . . .

Asking about Want–Desire
Would you like _____?
Do you want _____?

Would you care for _____?

Apologizing
I'm sorry.
I apologize.
Please accept my apology.
Please forgive me.

Intention
I'm planning to _____.
I'm going to _____.
I intend to _____.

Certainty
Are you sure?
Are you positive?
Are you certain?

Absolutely!
Definitely!
Positively!

Now Leaving Exit 6 Construction Area

☐ **Sequence of Tenses**
☐ **Reported Speech**
☐ **Noun Clauses**
☐ **One/Ones**
☐ **Tense Review**
☐ **Short Answers**

Sorry for the inconvenience. For more information see pages 188 and 189.

ExpressWays Checklist

I can . . .

☐ express dissatisfaction with products
☐ express dissatisfaction with services
☐ make requests of neighbors
☐ discuss housing repair problems
☐ complain about housing problems
☐ discuss employee rights
☐ discuss taking legal action
☐ discuss citizens' rights

REST STOP

Take a break!
Have a conversation!

Here are some scenes from Exits 4, 5, and 6.

Who do you think these people are?

What do you think they're talking about?

In pairs or small groups, create conversations based on these scenes and act them out.

Exit 7

FRIENDS, FAMILY, AND CO-WORKERS

Take Exit 7 to . . .

→ Agree with someone, using emphatic sentences and tag questions

→ Disagree with someone

→ Give compliments, using adjectives and question formation

→ Express opinions, using adjectives

→ Discuss television viewing, using adjectives

→ Express concerns, using *wish*-clauses and the present unreal conditional

→ Admit something to someone, using the past unreal conditional

→ Discuss important issues, using gerunds, *wish*-clauses, and *hope*-clauses

Functions This Exit!

Agreement/Disagreement
Likes/Dislikes
Admitting
Asking for and Reporting
    Information
Regret
Sympathizing
Wish–Hope
Complimenting

Lisa and Jasmin are having a discussion about something. Are they agreeing or disagreeing with each other? What do you think they're saying?

Alan and Karen are complaining about something at work that they wish were different. What do you think they're saying to each other?

A. You know . . . rush hour was awful this morning.

B. **I agree.**[1] Rush hour WAS awful this morning, wasn't it.

A. Traffic must have been slow because of the snow.

B. **That's just what I was thinking.**[2]

A. You know . . . this coffee tastes terrible!

B. **I agree.**[1] This coffee DOES taste terrible, doesn't it.

A. We should switch to a different brand.

B. **That's just what I was thinking.**[2]

---

[1] I agree with you.   That's true.   [2] That's exactly what I was thinking.
You're right.   I know.
That's right.

1 Business is very slow tonight. / The restaurant is almost empty.

2 It looks like it's going to rain. / We should have taken our umbrellas.

3 We should ask for a raise today. / I've never seen the boss in such a good mood.

4 Fred worked very hard on this annual report. / Let's consider giving him a promotion.

5 It's time to think about retiring. / We'll be able to spend more time together.

Agree with someone.

A. You know . . . they aren't very impressed with our presentation.

B. **I agree.**[1] They AREN'T very impressed with our presentation, are they.

A. I don't think we're going to get their business.

B. **That's just what I was thinking.**[2]

[1] I agree with you.
You're right.
That's right.
That's true.
I know.

[2] That's exactly what I was thinking.

Constructions Ahead!

> Traffic was awful today, **wasn't it.**
> Barbara is very helpful, **isn't she.**
> This report looks good, **doesn't it.**
> Thomas helped a lot, **didn't he.**
>
> He doesn't work here, **does he.**
> They didn't finish their work, **did they.**
> We shouldn't leave now, **should we.**

1. Dinner was delicious, ___wasn't it___.

2. Elizabeth seems to be an efficent worker, _____.

3. These new desk chairs aren't very comfortable, _____.

4. Our neighbors haven't been very friendly lately, _____.

5. I did my homework a little carelessly, _____.

6. I didn't get the job, _____.

7. Robert looks very tired today, _____.

8. The weather isn't very nice, _____.

9. That really wasn't a very difficult test, _____.

10. You're going to evict us from our apartment, _____.

11. I guess we should leave the party now, _____.

12. You don't love me any more, _____.

Fill It In!

Fill in the correct answer.

1 I _____ with you.
- a. know
- b. right
- c. agree ⟵(circled)

3 You're _____.
- a. agree
- b. right
- c. true

5 That's exactly _____.
- a. agree with you
- b. what was I thinking
- c. what I was thinking

2 _____ I was thinking.
- a. That's right that
- b. You're exactly what
- c. That's just what

4 That's _____.
- a. right
- b. agree with you
- c. exactly

6 I _____.
- a. know
- b. right
- c. was thinking exactly

Matching Lines

_c_ **1** You aren't pleased with my work any more, _____. a. didn't you

___ **2** You've hired someone to replace me, _____. b. have you

___ **3** You're going to eliminate my job, _____. c. are you

___ **4** You haven't been honest with me, _____. d. did you

___ **5** You got fired today, _____. e. do you

___ **6** You didn't like my spaghetti and meatballs, _____. f. aren't you

___ **7** You want to end our relationship, _____. g. haven't you

___ **8** You don't trust me, _____. h. don't you

InterActions

With a partner, create a scene that begins with one of the eight lines above. Choose a line, decide who the characters are, and figure out what the situation is and how it gets resolved. Create and practice a role play, and then present it to the class.

A. You know . . . I think the air conditioning is broken.

B. Really? **I'm not so sure.**[1] **What makes you say that?**[2]

A. Well, it's unusually warm in here. **Wouldn't you agree?**[3]

B. No, not really. **I disagree.**[4]

[1] I don't know.
I'm not so sure I agree.

[2] Why do you say that?
What makes you think so?
Why do you think so?

[3] Wouldn't you say so?
Don't you agree?
Don't you think so?

[4] I don't agree.
I don't think so.

The air conditioning is broken.

It's unusually warm in here.

Something is bothering Larry.

He's been very short-tempered these past few days.

Leslie is going to be promoted soon.

The boss seems to think she's the best person in the department.

They're planning to announce a big layoff.

All the managers have been acting strangely the past few days.

Jane might leave the company soon.

She seems upset about her upcoming transfer to our office in North Dakota.

Donald has a crush on Peggy.

He spends an awful lot of time near her desk.

Disagree with someone.

Fill It In!

Fill in the correct answer.

1 _____ agree?
a. What do you
b. Wouldn't you *(circled)*
c. Don't you think

2 Don't _____ so?
a. you agree
b. you know
c. you think

3 Why _____?
a. you think so
b. makes you say that
c. do you think so

4 _____ you say so?
a. Why could
b. Wouldn't
c. Don't

5 I'm not so sure _____.
a. I agree
b. I don't think so
c. I don't know

6 I don't _____.
a. agree so
b. know
c. so sure

7 _____ you think so?
a. Are you sure
b. Do you know
c. What makes

8 _____ disagree.
a. I'm so
b. I don't think
c. I

9 What makes you _____?
a. sure so
b. say that
c. agree so

Listen 1

Listen and choose the best response.

1 a. I know.
b. No. I disagree. *(circled)*
c. It wasn't, was it.

2 a. That's true.
b. Wouldn't you agree?
c. It is, isn't it.

3 a. Yes, it is.
b. Why do you say that?
c. No, not really.

4 a. I'm so sure.
b. She isn't, is she.
c. That's exactly what I was thinking.

5 a. I know.
b. We do, don't we.
c. All right.

6 b. Wouldn't you agree?
b. Why do you think so?
c. Don't you think so?

Listen 2

Listen and decide if these people are agreeing or disagreeing.

1 a. agree
b. disagree *(circled)*

2 a. agree
b. disagree

3 a. agree
b. disagree

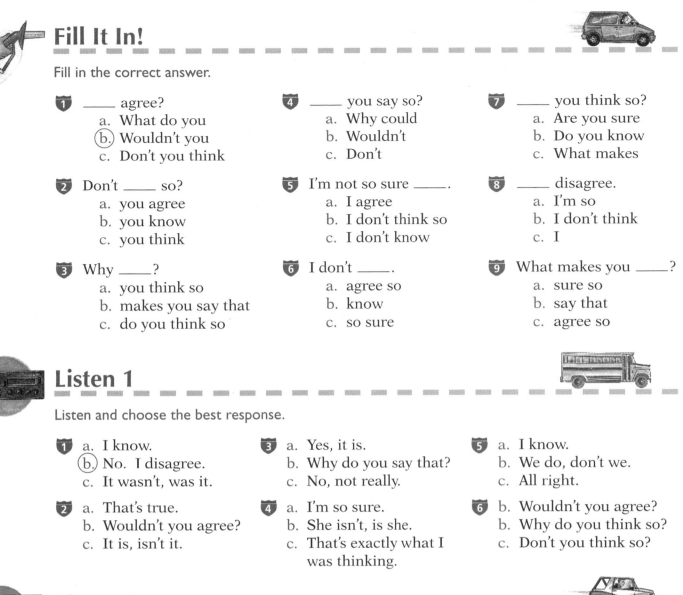

4 a. agree
b. disagree

5 a. agree
b. disagree

6 a. agree
b. disagree

REFLECTIONS
Are you an "agreeable" or a "disagreeable" person? Do you usually agree with other people's opinions, or do you disagree? When you disagree with someone, do you usually tell the person, argue, or keep your opinions to yourself?

Discuss in pairs or small groups, and then share your ideas with the class.

A. **I like**[1] your sweater. It's very colorful.
B. Thank you.
A. Did you make it yourself?
B. No. It was a gift from my sister.

[1] I really like
I love
I really love

Her sweater is very colorful. I wonder if she made it herself.

No. It was a gift from my sister.

His jacket is very nice. I wonder if it's waterproof.

Yes, it is.

His suit is very smart-looking. I wonder where he got it.

At "Gentleman's World" on Fifth Avenue.

Her new watch is very fancy. I wonder whether it's solar-powered.

No. It works on a battery.

1

2

3

Her briefcase is very impressive. I wonder if it's real leather.

No. It's vinyl.

His cologne is very exotic. I wonder what scent it is.

It's "Sea Breeze for Men."

Compliment someone.

4

5

ExpressWays

1. I wonder if her new watch is waterproof.
Tell me, _is your new watch waterproof_?
Yes, it is.

2. I wonder where he bought that tie.
Tell me, _____ ?
At Sears.

3. I wonder if they've decided on a name for the baby.
So, _____ ?
Yes. Oliver.

4. I wonder if he got the job at the bank?
Tell me, _____ ?
No, I didn't.

5. I wonder how he likes the used car he just bought.
So, _____ ?
It's a "lemon."

6. I wonder what the name of her perfume is.
Tell me, _____ ?
It's called "Angelica."

Listen

Listen and decide what the speakers are referring to.

1.
a. a wallet
b. shoes
c. paper

2.
a. the hiccups
b. a stuffy nose
c. cologne

3.
a. a boss
b. a fever
c. an aunt

4.
a. managers
b. earrings
c. a new restaurant

5.
a. an accident
b. a co-worker
c. a library book

6.
a. a calculator
b. a beach
c. a government

CrossTalk

Talk with a partner and then report to the class about your discussion.

Do you compliment people very often? What do you compliment them about?
How do you feel when someone compliments you?
What do you usually say in response to a compliment?
When someone compliments you, do you try to compliment the other person, too?

143

A. **How do you like**[1] my tie?

B. Your tie? Well, uh . . . I think it's nice.

A. You don't really like it, do you.

B. Well, uh . . .

A. **Please!**[2] Be honest with me!

B. Well . . . **To tell you the truth,**[3] I think it's a little loud.

A. Hmm. **You might be right.**[4]

[1] What do you think of

[2] Come on!
Listen!
Look!

[3] Honestly,
To be honest,

[4] You may be right.
That might be true.
That may be true.

Be honest with someone about something you don't like.

Matching Lines

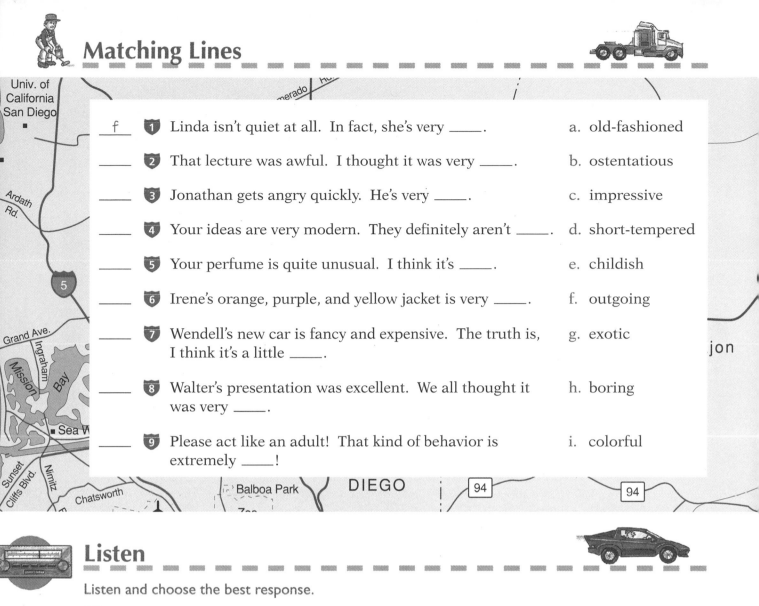

___f___ **1** Linda isn't quiet at all. In fact, she's very ____.

_____ **2** That lecture was awful. I thought it was very ____.

_____ **3** Jonathan gets angry quickly. He's very ____.

_____ **4** Your ideas are very modern. They definitely aren't ____.

_____ **5** Your perfume is quite unusual. I think it's ____.

_____ **6** Irene's orange, purple, and yellow jacket is very ____.

_____ **7** Wendell's new car is fancy and expensive. The truth is, I think it's a little ____.

_____ **8** Walter's presentation was excellent. We all thought it was very ____.

_____ **9** Please act like an adult! That kind of behavior is extremely ____!

a. old-fashioned

b. ostentatious

c. impressive

d. short-tempered

e. childish

f. outgoing

g. exotic

h. boring

i. colorful

Listen

Listen and choose the best response.

1   a. Thank you.
  (b.) Hmm. That may be true.

2   a. It's very impressive.
  b. That may be nice.

3   a. Thank you.
  b. Well, to be honest, it *is* a little short.

4   a. Hmm. Maybe you're right.
  b. Thank you very much.

5   a. Hmm. That may be true.
  b. I'm glad you like it.

6   a. I don't.
  b. To tell the truth, I think they're a little ostentatious.

CrossTalk

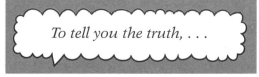

In the situations on page 144, the people expressed their opinions and told how they really felt:

> *To tell you the truth, . . .*

> *To be honest, . . .*

What do YOU think? Should these people have told the truth? Did they hurt the other person's feelings? What would YOU have done in these situations? Talk with a partner and then share your opinions with the class.

145

A. Did you see the new episode of "Pittsburgh Police" last night?

B. No, I didn't.

A. You missed a really good one. Lieutenant Morgan captured three bank robbers in an empty warehouse.

B. Oh.

A. **It's too bad[1]** you didn't see it.

B. **I have to admit,[2] I don't really enjoy[3]** crime shows.

A. Oh, really? Why not?

B. Well, I personally feel they're kind of violent.

---

[1] It's a shame

[2] To be honest,
To tell the truth,

[3] I don't really like
I don't particularly care for
I'm not really crazy about

Lieutenant Morgan captured three bank robbers in an empty warehouse.

1 One of the guests was a very funny comedian from Las Vegas.

2 They won by scoring a touchdown in the last few seconds of the game.

3 One of the contestants won $50,000.

4 He announced his new tax reform proposal.

5 Jennifer got stuck in the elevator of her apartment building.

Talk with a co-worker about a TV show you liked.

Your Turn

For Writing and Discussion

Tell about the kinds of movies and TV shows you like and dislike.

Listen

Listen and decide what kind of program these people are talking about.

1
a. crime show
b. comedy program

2
a. baseball game
b. game show

3
a. football game
b. game show

4
a. comedy program
b. press conference

5
a. cooking program
b. crime show

6
a. talk show
b. press conference

CrossTalk

Talk with a partner about your favorite television shows.

What's your favorite TV show?
What time and day is it on? What channel?
Why is it your favorite program?
What happened on the show the last time you saw it?

Report back to the class, and compile a list of everybody's favorite programs.

Class Debate

Watching television can be very beneficial.

Watching television can be harmful to people.

Divide into two groups – a group that thinks watching television is good for people and a group that thinks watching television is bad. With your group, make a list of all the reasons for the group's opinion. Present your group's arguments to the class, and listen to the opposing group's arguments. Then vote on which group's arguments are more convincing.

Reading: *Small Talk*

"How was your weekend?" "What are you going to do on your day off?" "How's that little boy of yours?" "Wasn't the traffic awful this morning?" "Did you see the Panthers game on TV last night?"

These questions, and the answers to these questions, are examples of *small talk* — the short, friendly conversations that people have with co-workers and friends. The topics of small talk may seem unimportant, but this type of communication between people is actually very important, especially on the job. By making conversation, people show that they are friendly and interested in each other.

The topics are simple. For example, people like to talk about the weather. The weather is something that affects all people, and it changes often. There is always something people can say to each other about the weather.

People also like to talk about their leisure time. On Fridays, in workplaces everywhere, you can hear people asking, "What are your plans for the weekend?" On Mondays, co-workers often greet each other by asking, "Did you do anything special over the weekend?" When talking about how they spend their free time, people often mention their family members. It is very common for people to talk with co-workers and friends about spouses and children. They share general information, such as children's sports activities, birthdays and anniversaries, and other family events. People don't usually share extremely personal information, such as family problems or personal finances.

Another common topic of conversation is television. People often discuss TV programs that were shown the night before: "Did you watch *Roommates* last night?" "What did you think of the football game?" They also like to share their opinions about the latest movies: "Steven Spielberg's new movie is excellent!" "I didn't think it was worth the price of the ticket!"

There are some topics, however, that are not appropriate for small talk. Examples of questions that are considered impolite and inappropriate include: "How much is your salary?" "How old are you?" "How much do you weigh?" "How much did you pay for your house?" These questions ask for information that most people consider too personal. Therefore, conversations on topics such as these rarely occur between co-workers and friends.

Small talk is important. However, some people don't like to make conversation about themselves or talk about topics they don't feel are important. They think that small talk isn't interesting and that it's a waste of time. But as a result, these people may be considered unfriendly, especially by co-workers who want to have good relations with people at the workplace.

Do You Remember?

Try to answer these questions without looking back at the reading.

1 According to the reading, small talk is ____.
 a. a waste of time
 b. very important *(circled)*
 c. extremely personal

2 An example of an appropriate topic for small talk is ____.
 a. age
 b. sports
 c. a person's salary

3 People who don't make small talk ____.
 a. show that they're interested in others
 b. are friendly
 c. may be considered impolite

4 People like to make small talk about ____.
 a. what they do in their free time
 b. prices they pay for purchases
 c. topics that are very personal

5 People don't usually make small talk ____.
 a. with co-workers and friends
 b. on Mondays and Fridays
 c. about family problems

6 Talking about television is ____.
 a. inappropriate
 b. an example of small talk
 c. too personal

What's the Meaning?

1 A person may talk about his or her *spouse*.
 a. activities
 b. husband or wife *(circled)*
 c. home

2 Very personal topics *rarely* occur.
 a. sometimes
 b. frequently
 c. seldom

3 Traffic was *awful* today.
 a. wonderful
 b. awesome
 c. terrible

4 Co-workers often *mention* their weekend activities.
 a. avoid discussing
 b. talk about
 c. whisper about

5 Some topics are *inappropriate*.
 a. improper
 b. approved
 c. correct

6 Small talk isn't a *waste* of time.
 a. good use
 b. bad use
 c. discussion

Cultural Intersections

Tell about differences between small talk in the United States and in your country.

When do people make small talk?
What do they talk about?
Which topics are appropriate?
Which are inappropriate?

We don't live in a warm climate.

We freeze all winter.

Our upstairs neighbors aren't quiet.

We aren't able to sleep at night.

A. You know . . . I wish we lived in a warm climate.

B. I agree.[1] If we lived in a warm climate, we wouldn't freeze all winter.

A. I couldn't agree with you more.[2]

A. You know . . . I wish our upstairs neighbors were* quiet.

B. I agree.[1] If our upstairs neighbors were quiet, we'd be able to sleep at night.

A. I couldn't agree with you more.[2]

[1] I agree with you.
You're right
That's right.
That's true.
I know.

[2] That's exactly what I think.
I feel the same way.
My feelings exactly.
[less formal]
You can say THAT again!

We don't work in a high-rise building.

We don't have a nice view of the city.

We don't have a vending machine with juice in it.

We have to drink coffee and soda all day.

We can't speak Japanese.

We need to hire an interpreter every time Mr. Hatano comes to town.

1

2

3

They won't buy us computers.

We have to use this messy correction fluid.

Management isn't responsive to employees' needs and concerns.

Morale is so low here.

Tell something you wish.

4

5

150

* I wish I/he/she/it/we/you/they were . . .

We have to wear our jackets in the office.

We aren't comfortable working at our desks all day.

Our lunch break is so short.

We don't have enough time to finish eating before we have to get back to work.

A. You know . . . I wish we didn't have to wear our jackets in the office.

B. I agree.[1] If we didn't have to wear our jackets in the office, we'd be comfortable working at our desks all day.

A. I couldn't agree with you more.[2]

A. You know . . . I wish our lunch break weren't* so short.

B. I agree.[1] If our lunch break weren't so short, we'd have enough time to finish eating before we had to get back to work.

A. I couldn't agree with you more.[2]

[1] I agree with you.
You're right
That's right.
That's true.
I know.

[2] That's exactly what I think.
I feel the same way.
My feelings exactly.
[*less formal*]
You can say THAT again!

This train stops at every station.

It takes two hours to get to work every day.

1

Our term papers are due this Monday.

We aren't able to go to the beach tomorrow.

2

The boss criticizes us all the time.

We don't enjoy working here.

3

Our English teacher explains every little grammar rule.

We don't have enough time to practice speaking.

4

Our dog and our cat fight with each other.

We don't have "peace and quiet" around the house.

5

Tell something else you wish.

* I wish I/he/she/it/we/you/they weren't . . .

Constructions Ahead!

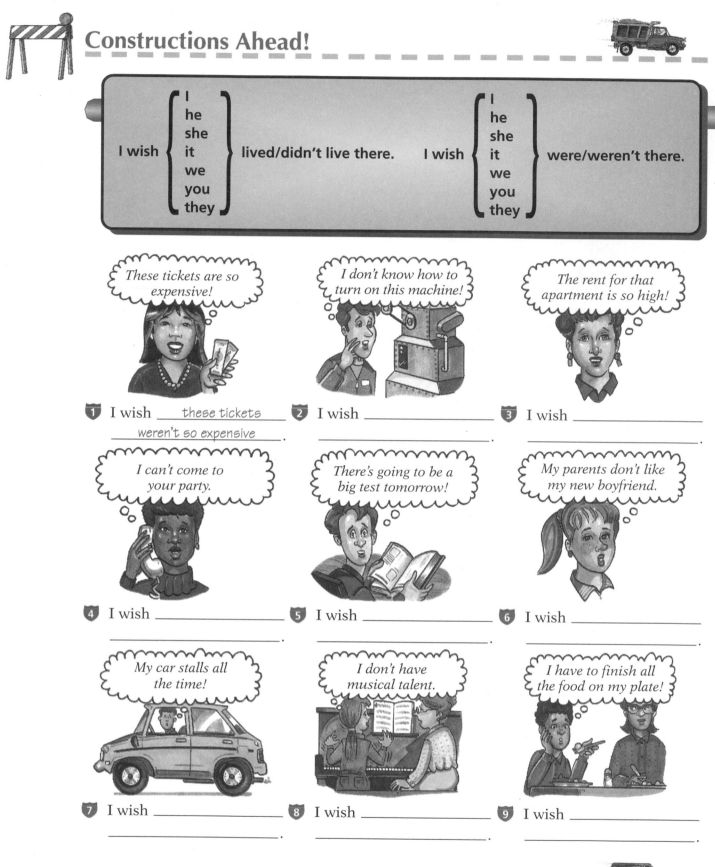

I wish { I / he / she / it / we / you / they } lived/didn't live there.　I wish { I / he / she / it / we / you / they } were/weren't there.

1. *These tickets are so expensive!*

I wish ___these tickets___ ___weren't so expensive___ .

2. *I don't know how to turn on this machine!*

I wish _____ .

3. *The rent for that apartment is so high!*

I wish _____ .

4. *I can't come to your party.*

I wish _____ .

5. *There's going to be a big test tomorrow!*

I wish _____ .

6. *My parents don't like my new boyfriend.*

I wish _____ .

7. *My car stalls all the time!*

I wish _____ .

8. *I don't have musical talent.*

I wish _____ .

9. *I have to finish all the food on my plate!*

I wish _____ .

CrossTalk

Talk with a partner about some things YOU wish, and then share your wishes with the class.

More Constructions Ahead!

(I would)	I'd
(He would)	He'd
(She would)	She'd
(It would)	It'd
(We would)	We'd
(You would)	You'd
(They would)	They'd

be happy.

If _____ would _____
If _____ wouldn't _____
(would not)

If I lived there, I'd be happy.
If I lived there, I wouldn't be happy.
If I didn't live there, I'd be happy.
If I didn't live there, I wouldn't be happy.

1. I'm not able to communicate with my husband's parents very well because I don't speak Italian. If ___I spoke___ Italian, __I'd be able to communicate__ better with them.

2. We won't buy that dishwasher because it costs too much. If _____ so much, _____ that dishwasher.

3. George isn't in good health because he refuses to stop smoking. If _____ to stop smoking, _____ in much better health.

4. Franco doesn't enjoy his English class. He says there's too much homework. If _____ so much homework, _____ his class a lot more.

5. Sally hasn't called, so I'm sure she isn't lost. If _____ lost, I'm sure _____ and ask for directions.

6. We don't see Grandma and Grandpa very often because they live far away. If _____ far away, I'm sure _____ them much more often.

7. I'm often late for work because the traffic on the expressway is so heavy. If the traffic on the expressway _____ so heavy, _____ late for work so often.

8. Barbara is the best person for the job because she always makes good decisions. If _____ good decisions, _____ the best person for the job.

9. You get a lot of cavities because you don't brush your teeth after every meal. If _____ your teeth after every meal, _____ a lot of cavities.

10. I'm sorry I won't be able to go to the dance with you, Henry, but I have a very bad cold. If _____ a very bad cold, _____ to the dance with you.

CrossTalk

The people on pages 150 and 151 are "griping." They're complaining about things they wish were different — at work, at home, and at school. How about YOU? Are there things in your life you wish were different — at work, at home, or at school? Talk with a partner and then tell the class about your discussion.

A. I wondering . . . Why didn't you come to the company's annual picnic?

B. The truth is,[1] I didn't know about it. If I had known about it, I would have come to the company's annual picnic.

A. I'm wondering . . . Why did you miss today's board of directors meeting?

B. The truth is,[1] I overslept. If I hadn't overslept, I wouldn't have missed today's board of directors meeting.

[1] The fact of the matter is,

Admit something to someone.

Constructions Ahead!

If { I / he / she / we / you / they } had/hadn't known, { I / he / she / we / you / they } would have/wouldn't have done that.

1 Robert, you forgot to take an important package to the post office this morning.

I'm sorry, but I had a stomachache. If ___I hadn't had___ a stomachache, I ___wouldn't have forgotten___ to take the package to the post office.

2 Jennifer, you missed the Girl Scout meeting last night.

Oh, no! I thought it was tonight. If _____ it was tonight, I _____ the meeting.

3 Timothy, why did you take a day off without permission?

I'm sorry. I didn't know I was supposed to ask. If _____ I was supposed to ask, I _____ a day off without permission.

4 Why didn't you call me when you came to town last month?

I didn't have any free time. Believe me, if _____ any free time, I definitely _____ you.

5 Why did The Great Panini miss today's matinee performance?

He was feeling "under the weather." If _____ "under the weather," he certainly _____ today's matinee performance.

CrossTalk

Complete the following any way you wish. Then share with a partner and talk about the situations.

I didn't know . . . .

If I had known . . . . I would have/wouldn't have . . . .

. . . .

I've Been Meaning to Ask You . . .

A. I've been meaning to ask you . . . Are you happy that you transferred to the Accounting Department?

B. Tell the truth, **I regret**[1] transferring to the Accounting Department. I wish I hadn't done it.

A. Really? Why?

B. Because the work is boring and the people in that section aren't very friendly.

A. **That's too bad!**[2] I'm sorry to hear that. What do you plan to do?

B. Well, I hope the Shipping Department is willing to take me back.

A. Is that likely?

B. I don't know.

A. I hope things work out for you.

B. Thanks.

> [1] I regret ____ing.
> I'm sorry about ____ing.
> I regret that I ____.
> I'm sorry that I ____.
>
> [2] That's a shame!
> That's a pity!
> What a shame!
> What a pity!

A. I've been meaning to ask you . . . Are you happy that you _____?

B. To tell the truth, **I regret**[1] _____ing. I wish I hadn't done it.

A. Really? Why?

B. Because _____.

A. **That's too bad!**[2] I'm sorry to hear that. What do you plan to do?

B. Well, I hope _____.

A. Is that likely?

B. I don't know.

A. I hope things work out for you.

B. Thanks.

You and a co-worker or friend are talking about something you regret. Create an original conversation, using the model dialog above as a guide. Feel free to adapt and expand the model any way you wish.

Constructions Ahead!

> **I slept** late.
> I wish **I hadn't slept** late.

> **I didn't go** to the meeting.
> I wish **I had gone** to the meeting.

1 I wish _____ last month.
   a. I've transferred
   b. I'd transferred *(circled)*
   c. I transferred

2 I wish _____ a used car from Honest Al.
   a. I haven't bought
   b. I didn't buy
   c. I hadn't bought

3 My son wishes _____ that scary movie.
   a. he won't see
   b. he hadn't seen
   c. he doesn't see

4 Mrs. Hogan wishes _____ more for the test.
   a. we had studied
   b. we had to study
   c. we study

5 My parents wish _____ a better student.
   a. I am
   b. I was
   c. I were

6 We wish _____ more time to spend with you.
   a. we have
   b. we'd had
   c. we'll have

7 I wish _____ the party so early.
   a. she had left
   b. she left
   c. she hadn't left

8 My whole family wishes _____ .
   a. I am married
   b. I were married
   c. I won't get married

> I hope { I / we / you / they } get an award.

> I hope { he / she } gets an award.

9 I hope _____ on time.
   a. she'll arrive
   b. she'd arrive
   c. she arrives

10 I hope _____ to the party.
   a. they come
   b. they'll come
   c. they'd come

11 We hope your team _____ .
   a. will win
   b. could win
   c. wins

12 She hopes _____ a raise soon.
   a. she got
   b. she gets
   c. she'd gotten

13 I hope the weather _____ fine.
   a. had been
   b. may be
   c. is

14 I hope this medicine _____ .
   a. helps
   b. will help
   c. would help

15 We hope _____ satisfied.
   a. you'd be
   b. you're
   c. you could be

16 Charles hopes _____ his sink soon.
   a. the landlord will fix
   b. the landlord fixed
   c. the landlord fixes

Looking Back

Asking about Agreement
Wouldn't you agree?
Wouldn't you say so?
Don't you agree?
Don't you think so?

Agreeing
I agree.
I agree with you.
You're right.
That's right.
That's true.
I know.
That's just what I was thinking.
That's exactly what I was thinking.
I couldn't agree with you more.
That's exactly what I think.
I feel the same way.
My feelings exactly.

[less formal]
You can say THAT again!
You might be right.
You may be right.
That might be true.
That may be true.

Disagreeing
I'm not so sure.
I don't know.
I'm not so sure I agree.
I disagree.
I don't agree.
I don't think so.

Asking about Likes
How do you like ____?
What do you think of ____?

Expressing Likes
I like ____.
I really like ____.
I love ____.
I really love ____.

Expressing Dislikes
I don't really enjoy ____.
I don't really like ____.
I don't particularly care for ____.
I'm not really crazy about ____.

Admitting
I have to admit, . . .
To tell the truth, . . .
To tell you the truth, . . .
Honestly, . . .
To be honest, . . .
The truth is, . . .
The fact of the matter is, . . .

Asking for Information
What makes you say that?
Why do you say that?
What makes you think so?
Why do you think so?

Regret
It's too bad ____.
It's a shame ____.
I regret ____ing.
I'm sorry about ____ing.
I regret that I ____.
I'm sorry that I ____.

Sympathizing
That's too bad!
That's a shame!
That's a pity!
What a shame!
What a pity!

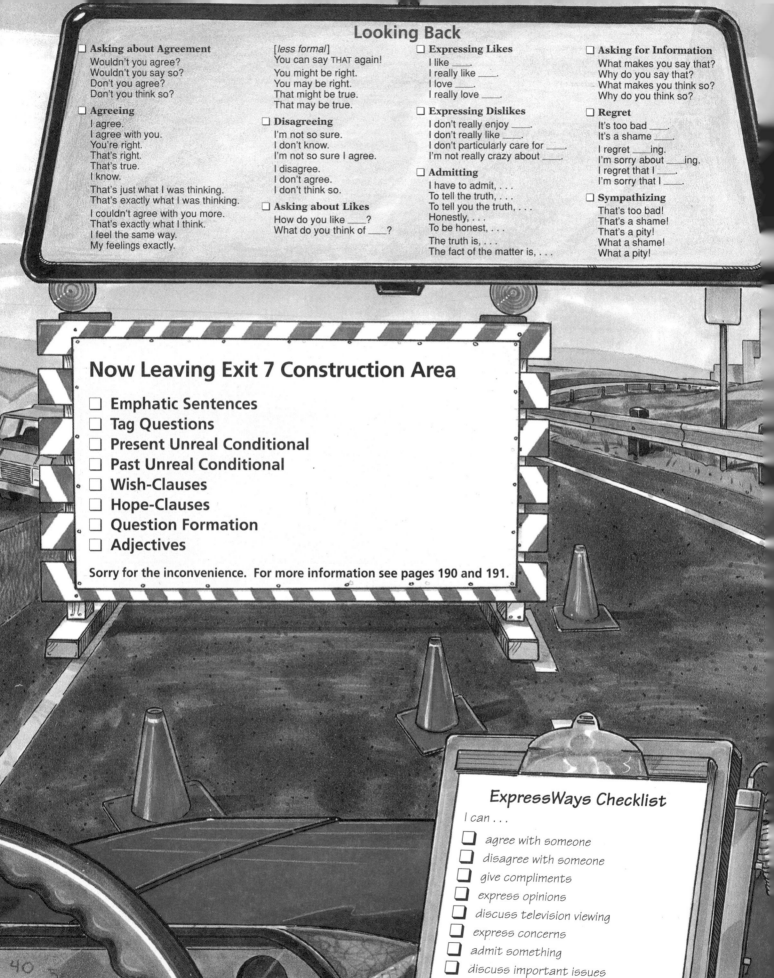

Now Leaving Exit 7 Construction Area

☐ **Emphatic Sentences**
☐ **Tag Questions**
☐ **Present Unreal Conditional**
☐ **Past Unreal Conditional**
☐ **Wish-Clauses**
☐ **Hope-Clauses**
☐ **Question Formation**
☐ **Adjectives**

Sorry for the inconvenience. For more information see pages 190 and 191.

ExpressWays Checklist
I can . . .

☐ agree with someone
☐ disagree with someone
☐ give compliments
☐ express opinions
☐ discuss television viewing
☐ express concerns
☐ admit something
☐ discuss important issues

158

Exit 8

STRATEGIES FOR COMMUNICATING SAYING GOOD-BYE

Take Exit 8 to . . .

➤ Initiate conversations, using tag questions and short answers

➤ Politely interrupt people

➤ Ask for and give clarification

➤ Clarify statements, using reported speech and sequence of tenses

➤ Say good-bye to someone by expressing obligation

➤ Express opinions about controversial issues

Functions This Exit!

Clarification
Interrupting
Focusing Attention
Agreement/Disagreement
Asking for Repetition
Leave Taking
Obligation
Checking and Indicating
  Understanding
Asking for and Reporting
  Information

Two strangers are talking at a bus stop. What do you think they're saying to each other?

Rachel just realized what time it is. It's late! She's got to go! What do you think Rachel and her friend Steven are saying to each other?

A. Traffic is terrible today, isn't it.

B. Excuse me?[1]

A. I was just saying traffic is terrible today.

B. Oh, yes. It is.

---

[1] Pardon me?
Pardon?
What did you say?
What was that?

"Strike up" a conversation with a stranger.

ExpressWays

1. The shopping mall is very crowded today!
   I agree. It is _____.

2. There are too many cars in this parking lot!
   You're right. _____.

3. Those muffins look delicious!
   Mmm. _____.

4. Our waitress is very helpful.
   You're right. _____.

5. The actors seem particularly nervous tonight.
   I agree. _____.

6. I think we should avoid making eye contact with that dog.
   I agree. _____.

Listen

Listen and choose the correct ending.

1. a. doesn't it.
   b. don't it.
   c. isn't it.

2. a. aren't there.
   b. are there.
   c. don't they.

3. a. hasn't it.
   b. isn't it.
   c. doesn't it.

4. a. hasn't it.
   b. isn't it.
   c. aren't they.

5. a. isn't there.
   b. aren't they.
   c. aren't there.

6. a. doesn't it.
   b. isn't it.
   c. has it.

7. a. doesn't she.
   b. isn't she.
   c. isn't there.

8. a. isn't it.
   b. doesn't it.
   c. isn't there.

Cultural Intersections

The people on page 160 are "striking up" conversations with strangers, as a way of being friendly and saying hello. Does this happen in your country? Do people have these types of conversations with strangers? If they do, where does this happen? What do people say to each other?

A. Excuse me for interrupting,[1] but your mother is here to see you.

B. Did you say[2] my brother?

A. No. Your mother.

B. Oh, okay. Thank you.

[1] Forgive me for interrupting,
I'm sorry for interrupting,
Sorry for interrupting,
I'm sorry to interrupt,
Sorry to interrupt,

[2] Was that

Politely interrupt two people who are talking.

Fill It In!

Fill in the correct answer.

1 ____, but I have to interrupt.
   a. Excuse
   (b.) Sorry
   c. Forgive

4 Did you ____ time to go home?
   a. say it's
   b. know
   c. interrupt

2 I'm ____ interrupting, but I need your help.
   a. sorry to
   b. forgive me for
   c. sorry for

5 Sorry to ____, but I have a question.
   a. excuse
   b. apologize
   c. interrupt

3 I'm sorry. What ____ that?
   a. did you say
   b. was
   c. was saying

6 ____ me for interrupting, but there's a problem.
   a. Sorry
   b. Forgive
   c. I excuse

Listen

Listen to each conversation and answer the questions.

Conversation 1

1 Where does this conversation take place?
   a. in a butcher shop
   (b.) in an office
   c. in a parking garage

2 Who is here for the meeting?
   a. Mr. Johnson
   b. Mr. Jones
   c. Mr. Jansen

Conversation 2

3 Where does this conversation take place?
   a. in a library
   b. in a drug store
   c. in a restaurant

4 Where is the problem?
   a. Table 5
   b. Table 9
   c. Tables 5 and 9

Conversation 3

5 Where does this conversation take place?
   a. in a classroom
   b. in an airport
   c. in a factory

6 What gate does the person want?
   a. Gate 10
   b. Gate 20
   c. Gate 12

Conversation 4

7 Where does this conversation take place?
   a. in a hospital
   b. at a ballgame
   c. in a biology class

8 Where is the problem?
   a. Room 350
   b. Room 315
   c. Room 355

CrossTalk

Do you think it's appropriate to interrupt people while they're speaking? Talk with a partner. Then compare your thoughts with other students' opinions.

A. Next year's budget does not include funds for your position.

B. I'm afraid I'm not following you.[1]

A. What I'm saying is[2] we're going to have to fire you.

B. Oh, now I understand.[3]

---

[1] I'm not really sure what you're getting at.
[*more direct*]
What do you mean?
What does that mean?

[2] What I'm trying to say is
What I mean is
What that means is

[3] I follow you.
I see.

"We're going to have to fire you."

1 "You're in perfect health."

2 "We lost a lot of money."

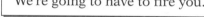

3 "I want to marry you."

4 "We have to lay off half of our workers."

5 "You flunked."

Clarify something for somebody.

What's the Meaning?

Choose the best answer.

1

> My test results were negative.

a. There weren't any results.
b. I'm fine. *(circled)*
c. I've got some medical problems.

2

> What are you getting at?

a. Where are you going?
b. What are you trying to get?
c. What do you mean?

3

> Your progress has been above our expectations.

a. You've done better than we thought you'd do.
b. We're waiting to see how you'll do.
c. You're taller than we thought.

4

> We've been out of touch for almost five years.

a. It's been five years since we've talked.
b. We haven't touched each other in five years.
c. We've known each other for five years.

5

> I don't get it.

a. I don't want to buy it.
b. I don't understand.
c. I don't have it.

REFLECTIONS

Sometimes people don't say things as directly or clearly as they could. Who does this? In what situations? Think about times when you have done this or experienced this. What were the situations?

Discuss in pairs or small groups, and then share your ideas with the class.

Matching Lines

Try to guess what the following expressions mean.

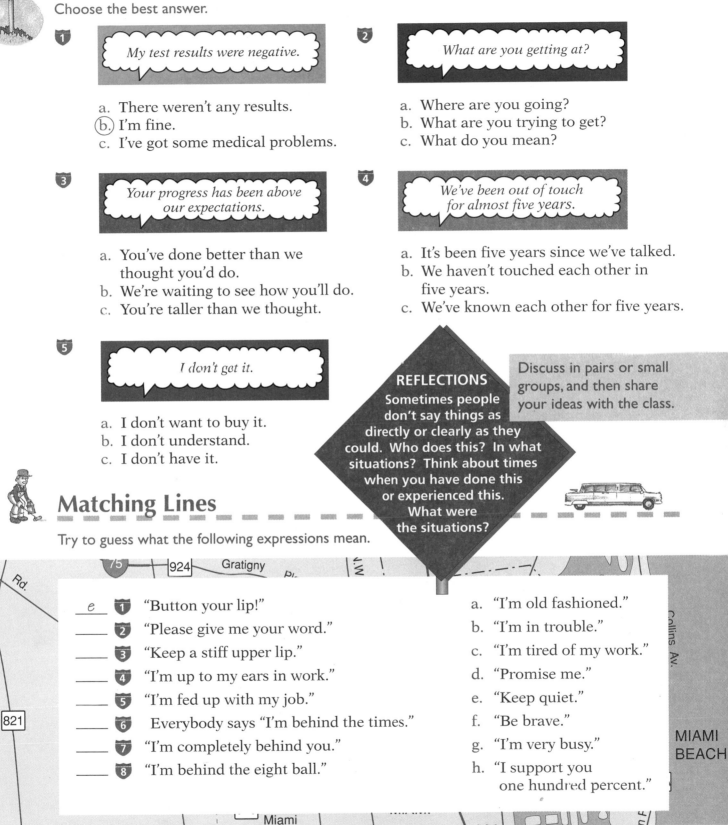

_e_ **1** "Button your lip!"
____ **2** "Please give me your word."
____ **3** "Keep a stiff upper lip."
____ **4** "I'm up to my ears in work."
____ **5** "I'm fed up with my job."
____ **6** Everybody says "I'm behind the times."
____ **7** "I'm completely behind you."
____ **8** "I'm behind the eight ball."

a. "I'm old fashioned."
b. "I'm in trouble."
c. "I'm tired of my work."
d. "Promise me."
e. "Keep quiet."
f. "Be brave."
g. "I'm very busy."
h. "I support you one hundred percent."

Figure It Out!

Think of other expressions you know, either in English or in your native language. Can other students in the class figure out what these expressions mean?

A. Our sales have been very disappointing this year.

B. **What you're saying is**[1] you're going to cut my salary.

A. No. **That's not true.**[2] I didn't say I was going to cut your salary. I just said our sales had been very disappointing this year.

B. Oh.

---

[1] What you're really saying is
What you're trying to say is
What you mean is
In other words,

[2] That's wrong.
You're mistaken.

1

2

3

4

5

Missing Lines

What do you think these people are saying? With a partner, continue these conversations any way you wish. Then present them to the class.

1. It seems a little cool in here. — What you're saying is . . . .

2. It's been a long time since we've talked. — What you're trying to say is . . . .

3. It's getting late. — In other words, ...

4. The food at this restaurant has been a little disappointing lately. — What you're really saying is . . . .

5. This bill from Blake's Department Store is a little high. — What you mean is . . . .

6. That new tie is very different. — What you're trying to say is . . . .

7. The Valentine decorations you put up are very bright. — In other words, ...

8. I'm not ready for a long-term relationship. — What you mean is . . . .

Community Connections

Look in newspapers and magazines for interesting advertisements or headlines and cut them out. With a partner, try to suggest ways of restating and clarifying the information.

I've Really Got to Go Now

A. By the way . . . **What time is it?**[1]
B. It's almost 6:00.
A. 6:00?! I didn't realize it was so late!
B. I didn't either.
A. **I've got to go now.**[2] **I have to**[3] catch my bus.
B. Oh! You'd better hurry! See you soon.

[1] Do you have the time?
Do you know what time it is?

[2] I've got to be going now.
I have to go now.
I'd better go now.
I have to run
I've got to run.
I have to get going.
I've got to get going.

[3] I've got to
I need to

It's almost 6:00.

catch my bus

It's about 1:30.

1 get to an important meeting

It's a little before 5:00.

2 mail these packages by 5 P.M.

It's exactly 2:45.

3 pick up my wife at the airport

It's nearly 9:00.

4 get my car out of the garage before it closes

It's close to 7:00.

5 take Rex home and feed him dinner

It's late! You've got to go now. Finish a conversation and leave.

Fill It In!

Fill in the correct answer.

1 I've _____ now.
   a. better go
   b. got to get
   c. got to be going *(circled)*

2 _____ what time it is?
   a. Do you have
   b. Is it
   c. Do you know

3 I _____ to run.
   a. need
   b. got
   c. better

4 _____ have to go.
   a. I've
   b. I'd better
   c. I

5 _____ you later.
   a. I'd see
   b. I'll see
   c. I see

6 I've got to _____ now.
   a. better go
   b. going
   c. go

7 What time _____?
   a. it is
   b. do you have
   c. you got

8 _____ got to get going.
   a. I've
   b. I'd better
   c. I

9 Do you have _____?
   a. get going
   b. what time is it
   c. the time

What's the Answer?

1
I'll see you tomorrow.
   a. Okay. *(circled)*
   b. Yes, I will.
   c. No.

2
What time is it?
   a. Soon.
   b. Almost 5:00.
   c. It's at 4:00.

3
I've really got to go now.
   a. I have to get going.
   b. Okay. See you soon.
   c. By the way.

4
I didn't realize it was so late.
   a. I don't.
   b. I didn't know.
   c. I didn't either.

5
I've got to get to the bank before it closes.
   a. You'd better hurry.
   b. I don't either.
   c. It's almost 4:00?!

6
It's 5:30.
   a. 5:30.
   b. 5:30?!
   c. What time is it?

Survey

For the next several days, watch people in your community as they say good-bye. What expressions do they use? What reasons do they give for saying good-bye? Report back to the class and compare everybody's findings.

A. It's been really nice seeing you again.

B. Yes, it has. I'm glad we had a chance to talk.

A. So am I. You know, I think I should **be going**[1] now. **I've got to**[2] pick up my daughter at the day-care center.

B. Well . . . **Let's keep in touch.**[3]

A. Okay. I'll call you.

B. **Take it easy.**[4]

A. **Good-bye.**[5]

[1] get going
be on my way

[2] I have to
I need to
I'm supposed to

[3] Let's stay in touch.
Let's get together soon.

[4] Take care.

[5] Bye.
Bye-bye.
So long.

pick up my daughter at the day-care center

1 be at work an hour early

2 get to my English class

3 meet an important client back at the office

4 get to the bank before it closes

5 get over to the ABC* studios for an interview on the evening news

Say good-bye to someone.

*ABC = American Broadcasting Company

Fill It In!

Fill in the correct answer.

1 We've ___ get together soon.
    a. supposed to
    b. have to
    c. got to ⟵(circled)

2 Let's ___ in touch.
    a. get together
    b. keep
    c. need

3 I'm ___ be there by 7:00.
    a. need to
    b. got to
    c. supposed to

4 He ___ be there on time.
    a. got to
    b. has to
    c. supposed to

5 I ___ get going.
    a. got to
    b. supposed to
    c. have to

6 Take it ___.
    a. care
    b. so long
    c. easy

What's the Word?

Complete the conversation and practice it with a partner.

agree	either	That's	could	Let's	Take	was
get	nice	It's	should	had	I'll	You

A. Well, I guess I ___should___¹ be on my way.

I didn't realize it ____² so late.

B. I didn't ____³. I've got to ____⁴ going, too.

____⁵ been really ____⁶ seeing you again.

A. Yes, I ____⁷. I'm glad we've ____⁸ a chance

to talk. ____⁹ get together again soon. Maybe

we ____¹⁰ meet for lunch.

B. Okay. ____¹¹ a good idea. ____¹² call you.

A. Great. ____¹³ care.

B. ____¹⁴, too. Good-bye.

CrossTalk

The situation above is very typical in the United States. Two people meet, say hello, talk for a while, and when they say good-bye, they often promise to "get together soon." Do you think these people will actually call each other, or is this just their way of saying good-bye? Talk with a partner. Then share ideas as a class.

INTERCHANGE

It Seems to Me . . .

We had too much conversation practice and not enough grammar in our English class.

Grammar rules are the most important things to learn in a new language.

Conversation practice is much more useful than studying grammar rules.

It prepares us to really communicate with people.

A. You know . . . It seems to me that we had too much conversation practice and not enough grammar in our English class. **Don't you agree?**[1]

B. **I'm not so sure.**[2] **Why do you feel that way?**[3]

A. Grammar rules are the most important things to learn in a new language. **Don't you agree?**[1]

B. Well, **I wish I could agree with you,**[4] but **if you ask me,**[5] conversation practice is much more useful than studying grammar rules.

A. Oh? **Why do you feel that way?**[3]

B. It prepares us to really communicate with people.

A. Hmm. **That's a good point.**[6]

---

[1] Wouldn't you agree?
Don't you think so?
Wouldn't you say so?

[2] I'm not so sure about that.
I don't know.
I don't know about that.

[3] What makes you say that?

[4] I hate to disagree with you
I don't mean to disagree with you

[5] in my opinion,
as far as I'm concerned,
I personally think,
as I see it,
the way I see it,

[6] You have a point there.
I see your point.

A. You know . . . It seems to me that _____.
Don't you agree?[1]

B. **I'm not so sure.**[2] **Why do you feel that way?**[3]

A. _____. **Don't you agree?**[1]

B. Well, **I wish I could agree with you,**[4] but **if you ask me,**[5] _____
_____.

A. Oh? **Why do you feel that way?**[3]

B. _____.

A. Hmm. **That's a good point.**[6]

You're having a disagreement with somebody. Create an original conversation, using the model dialog on page 172 as a guide. Feel free to adapt and expand the model any way you wish.

Fill It In!

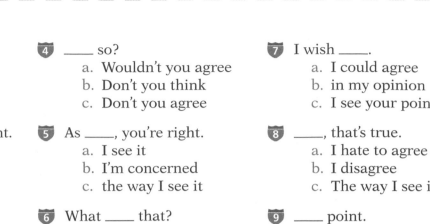

Fill in the correct answer.

1 I'm not ____.
   - (a.) so sure
   - b. agree
   - c. think so

2 If ____, I think you're right.
   - a. my opinion
   - b. I see it
   - c. you ask me

3 I don't ____ with you.
   - a. know about that
   - b. mean to disagree
   - c. so sure if I agree

4 ____ so?
   - a. Wouldn't you agree
   - b. Don't you think
   - c. Don't you agree

5 As ____, you're right.
   - a. I see it
   - b. I'm concerned
   - c. the way I see it

6 What ____ that?
   - a. do you feel
   - b. do you agree
   - c. makes you say

7 I wish ____.
   - a. I could agree
   - b. in my opinion
   - c. I see your point

8 ____, that's true.
   - a. I hate to agree
   - b. I disagree
   - c. The way I see it

9 ____ point.
   - a. You have
   - b. That's a good
   - c. I follow

Crossed Lines

Put the following conversation in the correct order. Then express your views about what these two people are talking about.

____ People who work all week need a day for shopping.

____ There should be one day a week when families can spend time together.

____ You think they should be closed? What makes you say that?

____ I don't know. What makes you say that?

____ Hmm. You have a point there.

____ Well, I don't mean to disagree with you, but the way I see it, stores should be closed on Sundays.

__1__ You know . . . I think all stores should be open on Sundays. Wouldn't you say so?

Listen

Listen and decide if the speakers agree or disagree.

1 a. agree
(b.) disagree

2 a. agree
b. disagree

3 a. agree
b. disagree

4 a. agree
b. disagree

5 a. agree
b. disagree

6 a. agree
b. disagree

7 a. agree
b. disagree

8 a. agree
b. disagree

Reading: *Expressing Opinions on the Job*

In some workplaces in the United States, the boss gives orders and the employees follow them. No one questions the authority of the boss. In other workplaces, employers give their employees certain limited opportunities to express their opinions. In companies that have suggestion boxes, employees write down their ideas on suggestion forms and place them in the box. In some workplaces, they submit these ideas anonymously. In others, they sign their names and perhaps receive an award for their suggestion. Many employers also have a policy that *the boss's door is always open*. When an employee wants to talk about a problem or offer a suggestion for improvement, the employer is always ready and willing to discuss it.

However, many people in the workforce now expect more than a suggestion box and a boss who is easy to talk to. They want a greater role in the important decisions that are made in their companies. They want to participate in the management of their companies and see their ideas put into action.

Many companies are responding by giving their employees greater responsibilities on the job. Some corporations have developed a participatory form of management, in which employees actively participate with supervisors and managers in the operation of the company.

Other corporations are reducing their various layers of management. They are cutting back on the number of top management positions, eliminating many middle management positions, and allowing more and more departments to manage themselves.

Some companies have adopted a team approach to participatory management, based on the successful Japanese management practice known as *quality circles*. These teams work closely together to identify ways to improve the operation of the company. This team approach is now popular in many companies.

More and more corporations are realizing that employee job satisfaction plays a very important role in a company's success. Therefore, they are adjusting their management styles to allow workers a greater voice on the job.

Cultural Intersections

Tell about workplaces in your country.

Are there opportunities for employees to give their opinions and ideas?
Do companies encourage workers to participate in decision-making?
What do employees expect from their jobs?

Community Connections

Visit a workplace in your community. Interview employees, and find out what opportunities there are for employee participation in decision-making in the company. Report back to the class and compare the results of everybody's "field trips."

Asking for Clarification
I'm afraid I'm not following you.
I'm not really sure what you're getting at.
[*more direct*]
What do you mean?
What does that mean?

Clarifying
What I'm saying is . . .
What I'm trying to say is . . .
What I mean is . . .
What that means is . . .

What you're saying is . . .
What you're really saying is . . .
What you're trying to say is . . .
What you mean is . . .
In other words, . . .

Interrupting
Excuse me for interrupting, but . . .
Forgive me for interrupting, but . . .

I'm sorry for interrupting, but . . .
Sorry for interrupting, but . . .
I'm sorry to interrupt, but . . .
Sorry to interrupt, but . . .

Focusing Attention
If you ask me, . . .
In my opinion, . . .
As far as I'm concerned, . . .
I personally think, . . .
As I see it, . . .
The way I see it, . . .

Asking about Agreement
Don't you agree?
Wouldn't you agree?
Don't you think so?
Wouldn't you say so?

Agreeing
That's a good point.
You have a point there.
I see your point.

Disagreeing
I'm not so sure.
I'm not so sure about that.
I don't know.
I don't know about that.

I wish I could agree with you, but . . .
I hate to disagree with you, but . . .
I don't mean to disagree with you, but . . .

Asking for Repetition
Excuse me?
Pardon me?
Pardon?
What did you say?
What was that?

Leave Taking
I've got to go now.
I've got to be going now.

I have to go now.
I'd better go now.
I have to run.
I've got to run.
I have to get going.
I've got to get going.

I should be going now.
I should get going now.
I should be on my way now.

Let's keep in touch.
Let's stay in touch.
Let's get together soon.

Take it easy.
Take care.
Good-bye.
Bye.
Bye-bye.
So long.

Now Leaving Exit 8 Construction Area

- ☐ **Sequence of Tenses**
- ☐ **Reported Speech**
- ☐ **Tag Questions**
- ☐ **Have to/Have Got to**
- ☐ **Need to**
- ☐ **Supposed to**
- ☐ **Short Answers**

Sorry for the inconvenience. For more information see page 192.

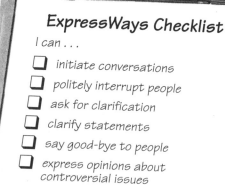

ExpressWays Checklist
I can . . .
- ☐ initiate conversations
- ☐ politely interrupt people
- ☐ ask for clarification
- ☐ clarify statements
- ☐ say good-bye to people
- ☐ express opinions about controversial issues

REST STOP
Take a break!
Have a conversation!

Here are some scenes from Exits 7 and 8.

Who do you think these people are?
What do you think they're talking about?

In pairs or small groups, create conversations based on these scenes and act them out.

Appendix

- Grammar Constructions
- Cardinal Numbers
- Ordinal Numbers
- Irregular Verbs
- Scripts for Listening Exercises
- Grammar Index
- Topic Index

Exit 1 Constructions

Embedded Questions

"Is there a post office nearby?"
Could you tell me **if there's a post office nearby?**
Could you tell me **whether there's a post office nearby?**

"When do they pick up the garbage?"
Could you tell me **when they pick up the garbage?**

I think I've figured out **what the problem is.**

Gerunds

Do you want any help **carrying** those
   grocery bags?
How about **turning** the valve?
I've tried **turning** the valve.

Infinitives

Could I ask you **to lend** me a cup of sugar?

Noun Clauses

I'm Jane, **your neighbor across the street.**

Time Expressions

Yesterday.
Yesterday afternoon.
The day before yesterday.
Last weekend.
This morning.
Two days ago.

Exit 2 Constructions

Embedded Questions

"Do you have flights between Chicago and Miami?"
I'd like to know **whether you have flights between Chicago and Miami.**
I'd like to know **if you have flights between Chicago and Miami.**

"What is our expected arrival time in Denver?"
Do you know **what our expected arrival time in Denver is?**

I'm calling to ask her **if she'd like to see a movie tomorrow night.**

Reported Speech

I asked you to fasten your seat belt.
I asked you not to play your radio.

Noun Clauses

I'm calling to tell him **his car is ready.**

Imperatives

Pick up the receiver
Please fasten your seat belt.

Time Expressions

at 3 P.M.
ten minutes **ago**
an hour **behind**
in an hour **or so**

Exit 3 Constructions

Embedded Questions

Could you tell me **if there's a monthly service charge?**
May I ask **whether you have an account with us?**

May I ask **where you work?**
Could you tell me **what the telephone number is there?**

Passive Voice

I think I've **been overcharged.**

Present Perfect Tense

We still **haven't paid** last month's telephone bill.

Time Expressions

Due **on January 15th.**

It isn't due **for a while.**

Should

Maybe you **should** stop at the bank.
How much **should** I get?
    You **should** get about eighty dollars.

Ought to

Maybe you **ought to** stop at the bank.

Have to/Have Got to

We **have to** buy groceries.

We**'ve got to** buy groceries.

Need to

We **need to** buy groceries.

Exit 4 Constructions

Impersonal Expressions with *You*

Are **you** permitted to park here?
Are **you** allowed to park here?
　　Yes, **you** are.
　　No, **you** aren't.

I don't think **you're** allowed to play ball in the park.

Reported Speech

She said you were doing poorly in social studies.

Could you **ask her to** excuse me from gym today?
Could you **tell him** I couldn't do my homework
　　last night because I didn't feel well?

Sequence of Tenses

*"Johnny **is doing** poorly in social studies."*
She said you **were doing** poorly in social studies.

*"Mark **got** into a fight today."*
She said you **had gotten** into a fight today.

*"Jennifer **needs to** have her eyes checked."*
She said you **needed to** have your eyes checked.

Embedded Questions

I was wondering **whether you're pleased with
　　Lucy's work.**

Should Have

I **should have** done better than that.
You really **shouldn't have** gone through that red light.

Could Have

You **could have** gotten a ticket!

Might Have

You **might have** gotten a ticket!

Must Have

I **must have** had my mind on something else.

Gerunds/Infinitives

I don't think **playing** ball in the park is allowed.
I don't think you're allowed **to play** ball in the park.

Short Answers

Yes, it is.
Yes, you are.
Yes, they are.
Yes, you were.
Yes, you did.
Yes, it has.

No, it isn't.
No, you aren't.
No, they aren't.

Exit 5 Constructions

Want + Object + Infinitive

Do you **want me to get** that man's car?

Present Real Conditional

If you don't, all the checks **will** bounce.
If you don't, we **might** get robbed.
If you don't, the motor **could** burn out.
If you don't, we **won't** be ready.
If you don't, we **may not** get their business.

Should Have

I **should have** gotten it a little while ago.

Could Have

I think you **could have** hooked it up a little better.

Present Perfect Tense

I **haven't written** up very many invoices since I started here.

Had Better

You**'d better** watch your step!
You**'d better not** block the doorway!

Short Answers

Yes, you are.
Yes, it does.
Yes, you do.
Yes, they do.
Yes, it should.

Supposed to

You're **supposed to** grease the pan first.

Exit 6 Constructions

Sequence of Tenses

"You're keeping all the neighbors up."
I had no idea I **was keeping** all the neighbors up.

"Our toilet won't flush."
I told him our toilet **wouldn't** flush.

"Can you fix it?"
I asked him if he **could** fix it.

"We don't have any heat in our living room."
I told him we **didn't** have any heat in our living room.

Reported Speech

"Our toilet won't flush. Can you fix it?"
I told him our toilet wouldn't flush, and **I asked him** if he could fix it.

"I'll get to it right away."
He said he would get to it right away.

Noun Clauses

I'd like to return this garden hose **I bought here last week.**

I'd prefer to exchange this one for **one that doesn't leak.**

One/Ones

I'd prefer to exchange this **one** for **one** that doesn't leak.

Tense Review

Simple Present Tense

It **sparks** when I plug it in.
The alarm **doesn't work.**

Present Continuous Tense

It**'s** still **burning** the toast.
It still **isn't working** right.

Present Perfect Tense

I**'ve been** very busy.
I'm calling to find out why you
    haven't gotten rid of the mice in
    our apartment yet.

Present Perfect Continuous Tense

How long **has** it **been sparking?**

Future: Will

We**'ll try** to fix it again for you.

Short Answers

Yes, he is.
Yes, it is.
Yes, you are.
Yes, it does.
Yes, it has.
No, it doesn't.
No, it won't.
No, it can't.

Exit 7 Constructions

Emphatic Sentences

Rush hour **WAS** awful this morning, wasn't it.
This coffee **DOES** taste terrible, doesn't it.

They **AREN'T** very impressed with our presentation, are they.
Roger **DOESN'T** look very well, does he.

Tag Questions

Traffic was awful today, **wasn't it.**
Barbara is very helful, **isn't she.**
This report looks good, **doesn't it.**
Thomas helped a lot, **didn't he.**

He doesn't work here, **does he.**
They didn't finish their work, **did they.**
We shouldn't leave now, **should we.**

Present Unreal Conditional

If we **lived** in a warm climate, we **wouldn't freeze** all winter.
If our upstairs neighbors **were** quiet, we**'d be** able to sleep.

If we **didn't have to** wear jackets, we**'d be** comfortable.
If our lunch break **weren't** so short, we**'d have** time to finish eating.

Past Unreal Conditional

If I **had known** about it, I **would have come** to the picnic.

If I **hadn't overslept**, I **wouldn't have missed** today's meeting.

Wish-Clauses

I **wish** we **lived** in a warm climate.
I **wish** we **didn't have to** wear our jackets.

I **wish** our upstairs neighbors **were** quiet.
I **wish** our lunch break **weren't** so short.

I **wish** I **hadn't done** it.

Hope-Clauses

I **hope** the Shipping Department **is** willing
   to take me back.
I **hope** things **work** out for you.

Question Formation

"I wonder if she made it herself."
Did you make it yourself?

"I wonder if it's waterproof."
Is it waterproof?

"I wonder where he got it."
Where did you get it?

"I wonder what scent it is."
What scent is it?

Adjectives

It's very **colorful.**
I personally feel they're kind of **violent.**

Exit 8 Constructions

Sequence of Tenses

"You're going to cut my salary."
I didn't say I **was going to** cut your salary.

*"You **want to** break up."*
I didn't say I **wanted to** break up.

Reported Speech

I didn't say I was going to cut your salary.
I said our sales had been very disappointing this year.

Tag Questions

Traffic is terrible today, **isn't it.**

Have to/Have Got to

I **have to** catch my bus.

I've **got to** go now.

Need to

I **need to** pick up my daughter.

Supposed to

I'm **supposed to** pick up my daughter.

Short Answers

It is.
It does.
There are.

CARDINAL NUMBERS

1	one	20	twenty
2	two	21	twenty-one
3	three	22	twenty-two
4	four		·
5	five		·
6	six	29	twenty-nine
7	seven	30	thirty
8	eight	40	forty
9	nine	50	fifty
10	ten	60	sixty
11	eleven	70	seventy
12	twelve	80	eighty
13	thirteen	90	ninety
14	fourteen	100	one hundred
15	fifteen	200	two hundred
16	sixteen	300	three hundred
17	seventeen		·
18	eighteen		·
19	nineteen	900	nine hundred
		1,000	one thousand
		2,000	two thousand
		3,000	three thousand
			·
			·
		10,000	ten thousand
		100,000	one hundred thousand
		1,000,000	one million

ORDINAL NUMBERS

1st	first	20th	twentieth
2nd	second	21st	twenty-first
3rd	third	22nd	twenty-second
4th	fourth		.
5th	fifth		.
6th	sixth	29th	twenty-ninth
7th	seventh	30th	thirtieth
8th	eighth	40th	fortieth
9th	ninth	50th	fiftieth
10th	tenth	60th	sixtieth
11th	eleventh	70th	seventieth
12th	twelfth	80th	eightieth
13th	thirteenth	90th	ninetieth
14th	fourteenth	100th	one hundredth
15th	fifteenth		
16th	sixteenth	1,000th	one thousandth
17th	seventeenth	1,000,000th	one millionth
18th	eighteenth		
19th	nineteenth		

IRREGULAR VERBS

be	was/were	been
begin	began	begun
break	broke	broken
bring	brought	brought
build	built	built
buy	bought	bought
catch	caught	caught
come	came	come
cut	cut	cut
do	did	done
draw	drew	drawn
drive	drove	driven
eat	ate	eaten
fall	fell	fallen
feed	fed	fed
feel	felt	felt
find	found	found
fly	flew	flown
forget	forgot	forgotten
get	got	gotten
give	gave	given
go	went	gone
grow	grew	grown
hang	hung	hung
have	had	had
hear	heard	heard
hit	hit	hit
hold	held	held
hurt	hurt	hurt
keep	kept	kept
know	knew	known
leave	left	left
lend	lent	lent
let	let	let
lose	lost	lost

195

make	made	made
mean	meant	meant
meet	met	met
put	put	put
read	read	read
ride	rode	ridden
ring	rang	rung
run	ran	run
say	said	said
see	saw	seen
sell	sold	sold
send	sent	sent
set	set	set
show	showed	shown
sing	sang	sung
sit	sat	sat
sleep	slept	slept
speak	spoke	spoken
speed	sped	sped
spend	spent	spent
stand	stood	stood
steal	stole	stolen
sweep	swept	swept
swim	swam	swum
take	took	taken
teach	taught	taught
tell	told	told
think	thought	thought
throw	threw	thrown
understand	understood	understood
wake	woke	woken
wear	wore	worn
win	won	won
write	wrote	written

Page 7

Listen and choose the best response.

1. Do you know whether there are any children in the neighborhood?
2. Would you happen to know where the nearest service station is?
3. Could you tell me whether you can park here?
4. Could you please tell me who I should talk to?
5. Do you know where I can find the superintendent?
6. Would you happen to know if they've delivered the mail yet?

Page 9

Listen and choose the correct answer.

1. A. Are you allowed to park here?
   B. Yes, . . .

2. A. Is it okay to play in the hallways?
   B. No, . . .

3. A. Are you permitted to hang laundry here?
   B. No, . . .

4. A. Is it okay to play music after midnight?
   B. Yes, . . .

5. A. Can you have pets in the apartment building?
   B. Yes, . . .

6. A. Are you allowed to throw newspapers down the garbage chute?
   B. No, . . .

7. A. Can you barbecue on the balcony?
   B. No, . . .

8. A. Is it okay to park here?
   B. Yes, . . .

Page 13

Listen and choose the correct answer.

1. Could you do me a . . . ?

2. Could I ask you to . . . ?
3. I don't want to . . .
4. Could you . . . ?
5. Could you possibly . . . ?
6. I'd be . . .

Page 15

Listen and decide which of the following is having the problem.

1. I don't know what to do. There's no heat coming out of it!
2. I've tried playing with the knobs on the back of the set, but it still isn't working right.
3. I've tried to jump-start it several times, but it still won't start!
4. Have you tried jiggling the handle? If that doesn't work, lift up the ball in the tank.
5. I've replaced the bulb, but it's still flickering and buzzing. What should I do?

Page 26

Listen and decide which statement is true.

1. First, dial "one." Then dial the area code. Then dial the seven-digit number.
2. First, insert your card into the slot. Next, enter your identification number. Then, indicate the amount you want.
3. Drop the money in the slot. Push the button that says "Pepsi." The can will drop to the bottom.
4. Pick up the receiver. Then put the money in the coin slot. When you hear the dial tone, dial "O."
5. Press down on the clutch and shift into second gear.
6. Insert the key. Turn it to the left and push.

Page 29

Listen and decide what place these people are calling.

1. I'd like to know what time Flight 64 is due to arrive.

197

2. Could you please tell me how much it costs to send a letter first class?
3. We want to make reservations for two nights.
4. I'd like to know if my car is ready.
5. I'd like to reserve a table for two tonight.
6. I'd like to reserve six seats for tomorrow evening's performance.

Page 31

Listen and finish the sentence.

1. He needs to get his air . . .
2. We don't want to trouble . . .
3. Six . . .
4. Are there thirty . . . ?
5. Could you tell me if that rink is . . . ?
6. Could you please reserve . . . ?
7. Is the café . . . ?
8. These two tables . . .
9. Would you please get the sticks . . . ?

Page 39

Listen and complete the message.

1. A. Mrs. Robertson isn't here now. May I take a message?
   B. Yes. This is Fred from Joe's Garage. I'm calling to tell her her car is ready.

2. A. Mr. Jenkins is at a meeting. Can I take a message?
   B. Yes, please. This is Jeff Carter of the Ace Corporation. I'm calling to ask him if he'll be in the office on Monday?

3. A. I'm afraid Ms. Rodriguez isn't available right now. Would you like to leave a message?
   B. Yes. My name is Arthur Wong. I'm at Washington College. I'm calling to tell Ms. Rodriguez I won't be able to keep my appointment tomorrow.

4. A. Tom Parker isn't in right now. Would you like to leave a message?
   B. Yes. This is Sally Langley from the Benton Company. I'm calling to ask him if he can change the time of the meeting.

5. A. I'm sorry. Mary Marx isn't in the office right now. Can I take a message?

   B. Yes. This is Barbara Baxter from the Personnel Office. I'm calling to ask her if she's free at 4:00 today.

6. A. Dr. Morgan isn't available right now. Would you like to leave a message for him?
   B. Yes, please. This is Officer Hall of the Westville Police Department. I'm calling to tell him someone has broken into his house.

Page 47

Listen and fill in the amounts of money you hear.

1. A. I'll go out and get some cash at the bank. How much do we need?
   B. Well, let's see. We need to buy groceries for the week. So we'll need about ninety dollars for that. And we're going to see a movie on Friday night. The tickets will probably be about fourteen dollars.
   A. That's right. And of course we'll need to pay the baby-sitter twenty dollars to watch the kids.
   B. And don't forget Jennifer and Michael's allowances for the week. That's another ten dollars — five dollars each.
   A. Well, I think that's it. That comes to a hundred and thirty-four dollars. Can you think of anything else?
   B. No, not really. I think that'll be enough.

2. A. Jim. I'm working on next month's budget. How does this sound? We have to pay eight hundred and fifty dollars rent and about forty-five dollars for gas and electricity. The telephone bill will be about twenty-five dollars. How much are we going to owe on our credit card?
   B. I think we owe about two hundred on MasterCard. And don't forget the insurance payment on the car. That's a hundred and twenty dollars.
   A. That's right. Oh, and we also have tuition at Tommy's pre-school. That's sixty dollars. So, all together that comes to one thousand three hundred dollars. Can you think of anything else?
   B. No. I think that's everything.

Listen and choose the correct date.

1. A. When is the MasterCard payment due?
   B. May 12th.

2. A. Have you paid the gas bill yet?
   B. No. It's not due until February 8th.

3. A. When did you send the check to the subscription department?
   B. On September 11th.

4. A. Did you remember to pay the electric bill?
   B. It isn't due until November 30th.

5. A. When is your appointment?
   B. It's at nine o'clock on May 3rd.

6. A. How long will you be on vacation?
   B. Until December 6th.

7. A. Have you paid the telephone bill yet?
   B. Yes. I sent a check on July 9th.

8. A. When is your wedding?
   B. It's on October 4th. I can't wait!

Listen and put the number under the correct bill.

1. A. I'm having trouble balancing the checkbook.
   B. Oh. I forgot to tell you. I wrote a check the other day for $83.50.

2. A. When is the bill due?
   B. It's due on August 15th. Don't forget to pay it.
   A. Don't worry. I won't.

3. A. Do you remember how much the bill was for?
   B. Hmm. Let me think for a minute. As far as I remember, it was for $27.70.

4. A. Do you happen to remember when the bill is due?
   B. If I remember correctly, it's due on November 5th.
   A. Thanks.

Listen and fill in the information.

1. A. May I help you?
   B. I think there's a mistake on my bill.
   A. Can you tell me your account number?
   B. Six-two-two . . . oh-five-six . . . seven-three-oh-one.

2. A. Customer Service.
   B. I have a problem with my latest bill.
   A. Would you tell me your telephone number, please?
   B. Yes. It's area code six-one-two . . . five-two-one . . . two-one-six-oh.

3. A. This is Rita. May I help you?
   B. Yes. Could you check my record? I'd like to know if my last payment was received.
   A. Sure. Could you tell me your account number?
   B. Yes. It's zero-three . . . two-one . . . six-two-eight.

4. A. I've been charged a penalty, but I paid this bill on time!
   B. Okay, sir. I'll check your record. Could you give me your account number?
   A. Let's see. It's five-three-two-nine . . . six-five-four.
   B. All right. Please hold.

5. A. What seems to be the problem?
   B. I've been charged for a long-distance call I didn't make.
   A. I see. What's your telephone number?
   B. Two-seven-six . . . one-two-seven-four.

6. A. I've been mistakenly charged a penalty!
   B. I can check your record. What's your account number?
   A. Four-eight-six-seven . . . two-one . . . nine-five-three-two . . . eight.
   B. Hold please while I check.

Listen to the question and complete the response.

1. Is fishing allowed here?

2. Are people allowed to take pictures?

3. Is it okay to park here?

4. Are you permitted to swim in this area?

199

5. Is hitchhiking permitted?
6. Is camping permitted here?
7. Are you allowed to ice skate on this pond?
8. Are people allowed to barbecue in the park?
9. Is it okay to roller skate here?

Page 71

Listen and put the number under the correct sign.

1. A. Excuse me, but I don't think people are permitted to smoke here.
   B. Oh. Thanks for telling me.

2. A. Look! There's a "No Parking" sign over there!
   B. Where?
   A. Over there.
   B. Oh. You're right.

3. A. I don't think you're allowed to make a U-turn here.
   B. You aren't?!
   A. No. Look. There's a sign over there that says so.

4. A. I think I see a sign over there that says you can't make a right turn here.
   B. You aren't allowed to make a right turn?!
   A. No. That's what the sign says.

5. A. Pardon me, but people aren't allowed to skate here.
   B. Oh?
   A. Yes. There's a sign over there that says so.
   B. Hmm. I didn't notice the sign. Thanks for telling me.

6. A. You know, I don't think we should be doing this.
   B. Why not?
   A. There's a sign over there that says "No Hitchhiking."
   B. You mean hitchhiking isn't allowed here?
   A. Not according to the sign.
   B. Oh.

Page 73

Listen and finish the sentence.

1. This time I'll let you go with just a . . .
2. Don't you know that making a U-turn on this street is . . . ?

3. This is a fifty-five mile-per-hour . . .
4. I really have to fix my . . .
5. Do you have . . . ?
6. I was only going . . .

Page 76

Listen and decide who is speaking.

1. What did I do wrong, Officer?
2. I see that your inspection sticker has expired.
3. You know, you really shouldn't have sped through that school zone.
4. I guess I just made that U-turn without thinking.
5. You were going eighty in a sixty-five mile-per-hour zone.
6. You know . . . you could have caused an accident!

Page 87

Listen and decide what is being talked about.

1. I'm disappointed. I really thought I should have done better than that.
2. Barbara works very quickly and always gets her work done on time.
3. I did well in every subject.
4. Walter arrives on time for work every day. In fact, I don't think he's ever been late.
5. I never expected to get such a good grade. I'm really pleased.
6. You know, I really could have done better than that.
7. Elizabeth is a very helpful employee. She always offers to help.
8. Mark is a very pleasant person who always does his job well. He likes his work, and everybody knows it.

Page 93

Listen and decide where the conversation is taking place.

1. A. Do you want me to take these letters to the post office?
   B. That would be great. I should have taken them earlier, but now I'm so hungry, I'd rather go to lunch.

2. A. Would you like me to put this blouse in a box?
   B. Thanks. That would be great. I bought it as a gift for my sister.

3. A. Do you want me to sweep up the sawdust?
   B. Thanks. I really appreciate it. I should have done it earlier, but I wanted to finish this before lunch.

4. A. I'm trying to do a printout of the report, but this machine keeps stopping.
   B. Maybe I can help you.

5. A. Would you like to order now?
   B. No. We'd like menus first.

6. A. Would you like me to get their car?
   B. Thanks. I appreciate it.

Page 95

Listen and decide where the conversation is taking place.

1. A. Did I write out this ticket all right?
   B. Let's see. It's Flight 83, and it leaves from Gate 46. Yes. You did a fine job!
   A. Thank you.

2. A. Did I set up the display all right? I haven't set up many displays before.
   B. You did a very good job! The cereal boxes and soda cans are just where they should be.

3. A. Mrs. Andrews? Did I gift-wrap these boxes all right?
   B. Yes, Robert. You did an excellent job!

4. A. Have I filled out the application correctly?
   B. Well, let's see. You missed one question. What's the purpose of the loan?

5. A. You put that motor together very well.
   B. Thank you. I'm glad to hear that. I haven't put together many motors before.
   A. Well, you did an excellent job!

6. A. I got that man's car and parked it at the entrance.
   B. Okay. I'll tell him.

Page 99

Listen and decide who's talking.

1. I just want to be sure. Am I doing the payroll the right way?

2. I think I could have fixed this bookshelf a little better.

3. I'd be glad to show you how to enter the data.

4. I need more adhesive to connect the pipes.

5. I'm supposed to do this printout first.

6. I'm supposed to give him an injection first.

Page 101

Listen to each conversation and answer the questions.

Conversation 1

A. Can you tell me where I can find tofu?
B. Sure. It's in the Frozen Foods Section.
C. Excuse me, Charlie, but that isn't quite right. Tofu is actually in the PRODUCE Section.
B. Oh. Thanks for calling that to my attention.

Conversation 2

A. I'm sure I have your paycheck here. Hmm. You spell your name K-R-A-F-T, right?
B. No, actually I spell it with a "C."
A. Oh. Thank you for calling that to my attention.

Conversation 3

A. How was everything this evening?
B. The food was fine, but the total on this bill isn't exactly right.
A. Oh?
B. Yes, sir. Actually, the total should be twenty-FIVE fifty, not twenty-SEVEN fifty.
A. Oh, I see. Thank you for correcting me.

Conversation 4

A. . . . And don't forget to study for the test on Thursday.
B. Excuse me, Mrs. Simon, but you said yesterday the test would be on MONDAY.
A. Oh, yes. You're right. Thank you for correcting me.

201

Listen and decide what's being talked about.

1. I'd like to return this. It's too difficult for me.
2. I need to return this. It's been opened.
3. I'd prefer to exchange this one for one that whistles.
4. I'd rather have one that's more powerful.
5. I'd prefer one that's portable.
6. I'd rather exchange these for larger ones.

Listen to the complaint and decide what's being talked about.

1. A. What's the matter with it?
   B. It runs too fast.

2. A. What's the problem with it?
   B. It plays the tapes too slowly.

3. A. What's wrong with it?
   B. It stalls when it rains.

4. A. What's the problem with it?
   B. It leaks when I turn the water on.

5. A. What seems to be the matter with it?
   B. The "A" and "Z" keys don't work.

6. A. Tell me what the problem is.
   B. When I turn it on, the picture is in color, but after one or two minutes, it's in black and white.

7. A. What seems to be wrong with it?
   B. The pieces don't fit together.

8. A. What's wrong with it?
   B. When I plug it in, it sparks.

9. A. What's the matter with it?
   B. It doesn't have enough memory.

Listen and decide which rule is being broken.

1. A. Timothy, I'm going to have to ask you to come in on July fourth to help take inventory.
   B. But, Mr. Wilkinson, isn't July fourth a holiday?
   A. I'm sorry, Timothy. I'm going to have to insist that you be here on the fourth. It's very important.
   B. I understand, Mr. Wilkinson.

2. A. Cynthia, I need you to work late this Thursday evening.
   B. This Thursday evening? Of course, Mrs. Anderson.
   A. Thank you very much, Cynthia. I'm sorry I won't be able to pay you for staying, but I'm sure you understand.

3. A. When is your baby due, Francine?
   B. In the middle of July. But of course I'll need to take some time off after the baby is born before I come back to work.
   A. Of course. You can stay out for one week and then we expect you back here full time.

4. A. Brian, you're really going to have to work harder and faster. I'm concerned about your productivity.
   B. Of course, Mr. Libertino.
   A. If you stop taking time off for coffee in the morning, I'm sure that will help increase your productivity.

5. A. Mike, we've run out of helmets. But don't worry. It's pretty safe here at the construction site. You really don't need one.
   B. I understand.

Listen and choose the best response.

1. That movie was great! Don't you think so?
2. You know . . . our new supervisor is very friendly.
3. I think we should work overtime this weekend.
4. Sally must be late because of the traffic.
5. Let's meet for lunch sometime soon.
6. You know . . . I think we need a new car.

Listen and decide if these people are agreeing or disagreeing.

1. A. I think George is going to get fired.
   B. Gee, I don't think so.

2. A. These french fries don't taste very good.
   B. You're right.

3. A. Our supervisor is in a terrible mood today.
   B. I know.

4. A. Let's have a surprise birthday party for Grandpa's ninetieth!
   B. That's exactly what I was thinking.

5. A. That was a wonderful lecture!
   B. I disagree.

6. A. I think we should start looking for another apartment.
   B. I'm not so sure I agree.

Page 143

Listen and decide what the speakers are referring to.

1. It's very nice. Is it real leather?
2. That smells great. I should get some for my husband.
3. He's been very short-tempered lately.
4. I like them! They're very exotic!
5. I think he has a crush on the bookkeeper.
6. I wonder if it's solar-powered.

Page 145

Listen and choose the best response.

1. Well, honestly, I think your shoes are a little funny-looking.
2. What do you think of my new ring?
3. You really don't like my new haircut, do you.
4. To tell you the truth, Norman, you could have typed this letter a little better.
5. I really like that new sweatsuit!
6. What do you think of my new earrings?

Page 147

Listen and decide what kind of program these people are talking about.

1. You should have watched it last night. It was really funny!
2. Believe it or not, somebody won $25,000!
3. They scored a touchdown in the last

minute?! That must have been an exciting game.
4. The prime minister spoke with reporters for over a half hour about the recent developments in her country.
5. Last night's episode was really exciting! Lieutenant Cook chased three robbers all over the city.
6. I stayed up until after midnight, but it was worth it. Jim Reno had some terrific guests on his show last night.

Page 161

Listen and choose the correct ending.

1. This report looks excellent, . . .
2. Our children play very well together, . . .
3. Since we've arrived here, the weather has been perfect, . . .
4. This baseball stadium sure is crowded today, . . .
5. There sure are a lot of students in this class, . . .
6. This hasn't been a very successful first date, . . .
7. Susan gives very good presentations, . . .
8. This coffee tastes wonderful, . . .

Page 163

Listen to each conversation and answer the questions.

Conversation 1

A. Forgive me for interrupting, Mr. Jones, but Mr. Jansen is here for the meeting.
B. Did you say Mr. Johnson?
A. No. Mr. Jansen.
B. Oh, okay. Thank you.

Conversation 2

A. Sorry to interrupt, but someone dropped a bottle of mineral water at Table 5.
B. Table 9?
A. No. Table 5.
B. Thank you for telling me.

Conversation 3

A. Excuse me for interupting, but which gate does Flight 10 leave from?

B. Gate 20.

A. Did you say Gate 12?

B. No. Gate 20.

Conversation 4

A. Excuse me for interrupting, but we need the emergency medical team in Room 315 right away.

B. Did you say Room 350?

A. No. 315. Right away.

Page 174

Listen and decide if the speakers agree or disagree.

1. A. You know . . . kids shouldn't have homework. They should play after school. Don't you think so?
   B. Well, I hate to disagree, but I think homework is important.

2. A. *Police Work* is a great show. I saw it on TV last night and really enjoyed it.
   B. If you ask me, it's the best show on TV.

3. A. I think American food is delicious. Don't you think so?
   B. I'm not so sure.

4. A. It seems to me that the teacher spends too much time on spelling.
   B. In my opinion, spelling is important.

5. A. As far as I'm concerned, we need to buy a new car.
   B. I don't mean to disagree with you, but I think maybe we should wait.

6. A. You know . . . we should leave for the airport now. There may be a lot of traffic.
   B. That's a good point.

7. A. I like this restaurant because the food is delicious and the prices aren't high.
   B. The service is good, too.

8. A. I personally think that dress isn't appropriate for a wedding.
   B. Really? What makes you say that?

GRAMMAR INDEX

TOPIC INDEX